LORD, TEACH ME TO PROSPER STUDY GUIDE

How To Discover God's Master Plan For Your Finances

JUNISE MOISE

ISBN: 978-0-9997745-2-6

DEDICATION

I would like to dedicate this book to my family for faithfully supporting me. They went above and beyond the call of duty as I wrote this book, helping me with household chores so that I could focus on putting pen to paper. I would not have been able to accomplish this endeavor without their unconditional support. You each have proven to me once again how you truly understand "it takes teamwork to make the dream work."

To my husband, Dominique Dukens:

I love you very much, and I thank God for sending me such a fantastic man of God. Thank you for being so supportive throughout this journey. Thank you for encouraging me to finish this project.

And to our amazing children:

Dominique, Elisha, Faith, and Junisa

Thank you for inspiring me, believing in me, and pushing me to follow the call of God on my life. Thank you for being my accountability partners.

ACKNOWLEDGMENTS

For the development and production of this book itself, I would like to offer a sincere thanks to:

- Pastor Kenneth W. Hagin, for allowing the Lord to use you to birth this book in my heart.

- My father and mother, Saint Juste and Micheline Mondestin, for loving me unconditionally and for teaching me how to serve God in my generation.

- My dear sister Mirlene Hans, whose encouragement helped me to fulfill my dream of writing this book.

- Christy Phillippe, my gifted and amazing editor and advisor, who transformed the book from its early stage to its finished product.

My dear friends and contributors who surrounded me and supported me during this journey: Ketty Duplan Giorgianni, Gail Lefiti, Rick Killian, Craig Sexson and Mary Sexson, and Minister Erica Moore, for inspiring me to step into my purpose.

INTRODUCTION

> *Thus says the* Lord, *your Redeemer, The Holy One of Israel: "I am the* Lord *your God, Who teaches you to profit, Who leads you by the way you should go."*
>
> —*Isaiah 48:17* NKJV

I was sitting in a church service, when my pastor read this scripture to the congregation and I could not believe what I was hearing. What a revelation! Did it really mean that I did not have to struggle to locate the road to success? That I could truly reach my destination if I allowed the Holy Spirit to be my Guide? I know the word prosper scares off some people; they equate the word with televangelists promising them millions in return for their giving. Unfortunately, some ministers have oversimplified the "prosperity message" and brought it down to apply to only the area of giving. I spent years listening to these various "prosperity preachers" share their own version of the "prosperity message," but unfortunately I never received the results they promised.

As I became more and more frustrated, I finally decided to go back to the manual—the Bible—and there I learned that God's prosperity plan covered more than just the area of financial giving. Giving financially is a great part of prosperity, but it is not the only prerequisite. By returning to the Word of God, I discovered that I had been missing some key pieces to my knowledge: I did not have God's complete master plan for my finances. I discovered that I could not follow someone else's plan and expect to reap the same results. I had to follow God's tailor-made plan for my finances. After years of searching, I finally found my answer in the Word, and my goal is now to share with you what the Lord has taught me.

Lord, Teach Me to Prosper emphasizes the importance of prospering in one's soul first, then it goes on to explain how you can prosper financially. My aim is to inspire you to action! God's desire is for you to prosper, not to merely live from paycheck to paycheck. This book will teach you how to receive a tailor-made financial plan from the Lord. God has a master plan for your finances, and He wants to share it with you. This book is for all of those who are struggling financially and for all of those who are tired of just having their needs met, and no more.

I am humbled that the Lord chose me to share this message, because I feel that I am the least of all candidates. I was born in a country considered to be the poorest in the Western Hemisphere. Many years ago, my family came to America with very few belongings. I myself came with my most treasured possession—a book—but as I learned about God's methods of operation, I learned that my birthplace did not have to keep me from my "wealthy place." I did not have to allow my beginning to determine my ending! When I accepted Jesus as my Lord and Savior, I experienced a new birth that provided me with a new beginning.

There are countless books on prosperity that line bookstore shelves, so you may be wondering, *Why do I need another book on prosperity?* But this book not only emphasizes how much God desires to prosper you, but it also teaches you how to receive God's master plan for your finances. You have been called to rise to a certain financial level that the Lord has for you, but you must be willing to follow God's instructions to reach the destination He has for you. You no longer have to abide in a financial desert; no, it is time for you to move on from that place. Let's embark together on a journey to your prosperous place!

Perhaps you have been waiting for this book. Have you been praying, seeking, and asking God, *Why is it that I feel so stuck and that I can't seem to progress financially?* The answer is found within this book. *Lord, Teach Me to Prosper* will provide you with the answers that you have been seeking. It will help you to experience the financial freedom for which you have been longing. You will learn how God prospers His children. And after reading this book, you will be confident enough to pray, "Lord, teach me to prosper!"

A HEARTFELT PRAYER FOR YOU

My prayer for you is that the Lord would use this book to change your life. I pray that the financial breakthrough you have been waiting on will come as you are reading this book. I pray that this book will not just be words on a page, but that it will be life to you. These are not simply my words; they have been inspired by the Lord. I pray that this book is the answer to your prayers.

CONTENTS

STUDY GUIDE

Many times, we quickly read through a book without grasping its concepts. My desire is for you to internalize the principles in this study guide so that you can begin to prosper. The purpose of this study guide is to bring clarity. As you spend time thinking, praying and answering the questions, you will gain a level of clarity that you have never experienced before. Do not rush through this study guide, take your time to ponder the questions. Joshua was told in the book of Joshua, "Keep this Book of the Law always on your lips; meditate on it day and night, so that you may be careful to do everything written in it. Then you will be prosperous and successful" (Joshua 1:8 NIV). To meditate means to engage in intensive thinking. I encourage you to embark on a prayer and fasting season to seek out wisdom from God. Grab your Bible, my book, *Lord Teach Me to Prosper,* and this study guide. Spend some time searching and asking God to teach you how to prosper.

Set aside some time to think deeply about the questions without distractions. Revelation comes out of meditation. This study guide is not about money, it's purpose is to help you gain clarity in every area of your life. Never make the pursuit of money your main objective. A prosperous life is a result of following the plan of God for your life. "Everything is possible for one who believes" (Mark 9:23 NIV).

Michelangelo said, "The greatest danger for most of us is not that our aim is too high and we miss it, but that it is too low and we reach it."

1

WHAT DOES IT MEAN TO PROSPER?

Thus says the L*ORD, your Redeemer, The Holy One of Israel: "I am the* L*ORD your God, Who teaches you to profit, Who leads you by the way you should go."*

—Isaiah 48:17 NKJV

I was amazed as I read this verse. Did God really want to "teach" me how to prosper? As I later read through the Bible, I discovered that the answer to that question was a resounding yes. Unfortunately, I continued to struggle financially for many years after discovering this verse, because I did not yet know how to fully apply it to my finances. I did not understand how to prosper. To *prosper* means "to succeed in material terms; to be financially successful." The Lord does, indeed, want to teach you how to prosper, and He desires for you to walk in abundance. Financial abundance is about the ability to make choices. Poverty limits you, taking away your power of choice. The Lord has a specific plan for your finances, but for you to discover that plan, you must be willing to pray, *Lord, teach me to prosper.*

TURNING POINT

There is a pivotal scene in the movie *Gone with the Wind*, in which the lead female character, Scarlett, makes a life-changing decision. She says aloud to herself, "As God is my witness, as God is my witness, they're not going to lick me. I'm going to live through this, and when it's all over, I'll never be hungry again. No, nor any of my folk. If I have to lie, steal, cheat, or kill, as God is my witness, I'll never be hungry again." As Christians, we do not have to resort to the tactics employed by Scarlett; we can trust God to be our Provider. Unfortunately, unless we reach this same level of frustration with the status quo in our lives, we will not take any action. We must become so fed up with our current financial situation that it causes us to change course and get on the path to financial freedom.

My own pivotal moment came because of a road trip. Many years ago, my family and I wanted to go on a trip to Florida, but we could not afford the plane tickets. We determined that our best option would be to drive from Arizona to Florida. Shortly after I began the long drive, I fell asleep at the wheel. The car was swerving out of control, with my kids asleep in the back. When I woke up, I saw chaos all around me. I saw rocks flying, glass breaking, and it was almost as if time stood still in that moment. I could not even speak out loud, because I was in such shock. The car hit the side of a hill and stopped suddenly. I was bleeding from cuts that I sustained from broken glass. The hill into which our car had crashed was located just a few feet from a ravine. Only by the grace of God, did we all survive that crash.

I spent a great deal of time analyzing my life as I healed from my injuries after the crash. I could not believe that I had allowed my finances to be reduced to such a terrible condition. How had I allowed myself to get into such a financial predicament that I could not even afford plane tickets? I decided that "as God was my witness," I was going to live through that, and when it was all over,

I would never again allow myself to get into such dire financial straits that I could not even afford plane tickets.

REFLECTION

1. What does the word prosper mean to you?

2. Do you believe that God has a plan for your finances?

3. Was there a moment in your life that birthed your desire to prosper?

4. Why do you want to prosper? (Study Luke 12:15)

5. Who is your provider?

ASK FOR THE MASTER PLAN

The Lord has a plan to prosper you, but you must receive His master plan for your finances before you can experience His financial abundance. It takes time to seek God's wisdom concerning your finances. I once heard a story of a man who became a millionaire in the middle of the Great Depression. Each time he was presented with an investment opportunity, he would spend time in his prayer closet until he received wisdom from the Lord. Many times, he would spend three days fasting and praying before he would even receive an answer from God. And sometimes the wisdom that he received went contrary to what the so-called experts of the world would have advised, but this man never lost any money on any investments by following this practice.

It is not easy to dedicate hours to prayer, seeking wisdom from the Lord. We live in a fast-paced world, so we often struggle to find time to be still enough to hear from God. We may wonder why God seems to favor other people while we continue to struggle just to make ends meet. It may seem as if the people around us always have something going on, while we continue to feel stuck in the same place. We may watch others prosper financially while we still struggle just to advance. Year after year, we find ourselves in the same financial position. We try to determine what we are doing wrong that is keeping us from advancing. The Scriptures say, "You do not have because you do not ask God" (James 4:2 NIV). When was the last time you truly asked God for help concerning your finances? God wants to favor you, and He wants to bring you from where you are financially right now, to where you need to be.

Isaac learned to follow God's master plan for his life, and he reaped the benefits as a result. The town of Gerar was experiencing a famine, and Isaac wanted to relocate his family to Egypt, where food was still in abundance. During a famine, there is an extreme shortage of food that can lead to mass starvation. Isaac, wanting to provide for his family, searched for the best opportunities available to him. He discovered that Egypt was still prospering, so he decided that he and his family would move there in order to escape the famine. But the Lord interrupted his plans and said, "Do not go down to Egypt; live in the land where I tell you to live. Stay in this land for a while, and I will be with you and will bless you" (Genesis 26:2–3 NIV). Isaac followed God's plan and stayed in the land of famine, and he reaped the benefits of his obedience: "Isaac planted crops in that land and the same year reaped a hundredfold, because the LORD blessed him" (Genesis 26:12 NIV).

Another man shared a story of how the Lord taught him to prosper. He was told in a dream to start a business in a field in which he had no experience. He was willing to do the same as Mary, Jesus' mother, told the servants to do concerning the instructions of Jesus at the wedding in Cana of Galilee: "Do whatever he tells you" (John 2:5 NIV). This man did not know what his next steps would be; all he knew was that he was to start the business. Out of desperation, he sat on a chair each day, calling on Jesus repeatedly, "Jesus…Jesus!" A week later, someone who had experience in that very field offered to teach him. He eventually succeeded in that business because he sought God's guidance each step of the way and followed His instructions. He became a financial success because he learned to follow the leading of the Holy Spirit.

REFLECTION

1. Do you struggle to find time to be still enough to hear from God?

2. Have you ever truly asked God for help concerning your finances?

3. How much time are you willing to invest in prayer each day?

4. Do you believe you are worthy of financial success?

5. Are you prepared to handle a new level of wealth?

GOD'S WISDOM TO PROSPER

We must receive wisdom from the Lord in order to experience success in every area of our lives. Wisdom is the application of knowledge; it is the ability to have a discerning heart. In the third chapter of 1 Kings, God visited Solomon in a dream in order to ask him a question: What did Solomon want most in the world? The Lord offered to grant any desire of his heart, and Solomon's answer forever changed the course of his life. Solomon asked for wisdom instead of riches, and as a result the Lord gave him more than he ever asked for.

> *Since this is your heart's desire and you have not asked for wealth, possessions or honor, nor for the death of your enemies, and since you have not asked for a long life but for wisdom and knowledge to govern my people over whom I have made you king, therefore wisdom and knowledge will be given you. And I will also give you wealth, possessions and honor, such as no king who was before you ever had and none after you will have.*
>
> —*2 Chronicles 1:11–12* NIV

We do not have to struggle to solve our own problems, because we can access wisdom from the One who created the universe. The reason that we sometimes fail to receive the wisdom of God is because many times we are simply too busy to hear. God oftentimes speaks to our hearts in a whisper, and if we are not listening attentively, we can miss it. We must learn to spend time alone in the presence of God. We must take the time to sit down and listen. One of my favorite scripture passages tells us to "be still, and know that I am God" (Psalm 46:10 NIV). Many times, we are simply not "still" enough to receive the revelation that He is God. We do not receive the answers that we so desperately seek, because we never ask God for wisdom in the areas of our lives in which we need direction.

REFLECTION

1. What is your definition of wisdom?

2. What is your greatest desire?

3. How much time will you dedicate this week to praying for wisdom?

4. What caused Solomon to prosper?

5. What is keeping you from receiving the wisdom that you need to prosper?

TAKE FINANCIAL TERRITORY

The secrets to your financial breakthrough are hidden in the Word. They are not hidden from you; they are hidden for you. God's prosperity plan is not complicated. The wicked prosper because there is no resistance. They do not deal with the same opposition as the children of God do. There is no hindrance from the enemy, no blockage to their prospering. But when the children of God attempt to prosper, the enemy tries to bring confusion.

Do not allow fear to fill up your heart. Some of God's children are so fearful of their bills, they are actually afraid of the numbers. Some are overwhelmed with the water bill, the electricity bill, and the gas bill. They act like the spies who brought back an evil report from the Promised Land. They say, "God, I know You told me to take my financial territory, but there are giants in the land. There is the insurance bill and there's the mortgage, and I can't overcome them. They are bigger than me—they are greater than me." We must look higher, because God is not intimidated by numbers. What is a water bill when compared to the amount of resources that He has at His disposal? Our bills are not comparable to God's resources.

A description of heaven in the book of Revelation states: "The twelve gates were twelve pearls, each gate made of a single pearl. The great street of the city was of gold, as pure as transparent glass" (Revelation 21:21 NIV). Heaven is full of abundance! We must expand our vision, expand our thinking. We must begin to dream a bigger dream and see a bigger picture. We must not be as the children of Israel, who did not enter the Promised Land because they were so focused on their limitations. They were only focused on what they could see with their physical eyes. They failed to look up, to see with their spiritual eyes. The story of Elisha and Gehazi illustrates the fact that there is a spiritual realm that we cannot see with our physical eyes:

> *When the servant of the man of God got up and went out early the next morning, an army with horses and chariots had surrounded the city. "Oh no, my lord! What shall we do?" the servant asked. "Don't be afraid," the prophet answered. "Those who are with us are more than those who are with them." And Elisha prayed, "Open his eyes, LORD, so that he may see." Then the LORD opened the servant's eyes, and he looked and saw the hills full of horses and chariots of fire all around Elisha.*
>
> *—2 Kings 6:15–17*

When the Lord opened Gehazi's eyes, he saw that he was surrounded by angels. When he saw that the numbers that were against him were smaller than the numbers that were with him, the fear left Gehazi's heart and he was filled with confidence. Fear can grip our hearts when we focus on the numbers. We can become so overwhelmed with fear when we pay attention to what is against us, instead of focusing on who is for us, who is with us, and who is in us. We will become emboldened when we put our focus where it belongs: on the Lord. We will boldly stare at financial lack and declare that it must leave!

This is your year of financial breakthrough. Many times, you have looked on the other side to financial freedom, and you have felt so close to it. But each time you tried to take a step forward, you have felt pushed back several levels. Today the Lord is removing the limitations from your life. He is removing financial roadblocks, so that you can go on to the other side. You will begin to write big checks, and you will become a great giver in the Kingdom of God. Many of God's children have had the desire to give but they have not had the funds—but you will now have the funds. The money is to fund the work of the Kingdom. You will be able to help others get out of debt. Do not forget the place from which God is bringing you. Do not be tempted to be stingy with the money He brings into your life. Give as you are led to give by the Lord, and be a big giver. Do not fear giving, because there is plenty more. You are being released from a fear of lack, and you are being released into your purpose.

REFLECTION

1. Where can you find the secrets to your financial breakthrough?

2. What is your biggest financial fear? Locate the scriptures that deal with that area.

3. What is your biggest financial giant?

4. Is God intimidated by a large amount of debt?

5. What kept the children of Israel from entering the promised land?

2

WHAT IS YOUR PURPOSE?

"For I know the plans I have for you," declares the LORD, "plans to prosper you and not to harm you, plans to give you hope and a future."

—Jeremiah 29:11 NIV

I spent so many years seeking—but I was seeking the wrong things. I spent so many years searching—but I was searching in the wrong places. I looked everywhere for answers. I wanted all of my questions answered: Who am I? Where am I going? What is my purpose? How can I become successful in my life? I read countless books and other materials, thinking that my answer would perhaps be found in a blog, an article, a book, or even in a podcast. But the longer I searched, the more frustrated I became, because my search was becoming more and more futile.

I never found my answers in any of these resources until I discovered that the answer was in The Book that had been right within my reach throughout my entire futile search. I discovered that I had access to the greatest Teacher ever, whose aim has always been to reveal the mysteries of the Bible to me. I had wasted so much effort seeking answers from the world, when the Holy Spirit, who lives inside me, was yearning—for all of that time—to share the secrets of true success. I had neglected the greatest Resource—and He was right inside of me!

Perhaps you have a hard time believing that your own prayers will be answered, because you think the Lord has to "find a way" to get the answer to you, as He did with Daniel. Perhaps you believe that the Lord has to fight to get His solution to you, just as the angel Gabriel fought for twenty-one days before he could get through to Daniel. But the difference is this: Daniel was not born again, and he did not have the Holy Spirit living inside of him but you do! Jesus has already fought the battle for you and He won. The Lord no longer has to fight a battle to reach you with the answers you need—because you have the person of the Holy Spirit living inside of you.

The Holy Spirit can speak to you at any moment. You have the Greater One living inside of you, and He has all the answers that you need for any situation that you face. The Holy Spirit can provide you with the strategic plan you need to accomplish success in any new endeavor. He can be your greatest business coach, ministry coach, or spiritual coach. Many of us are running after counsel from others while we neglect the greatest counsel—the One already living inside of us. Jesus said, "The Holy Spirit will teach you at that time what you should say" (Luke 12:12 NIV). I believe that is how the Holy Spirit operates: He stands ready to teach you what you need to know at any given moment. Many of us never receive His counsel, because we either neglect His presence or we do not ask for His help.

> *"But the Advocate, the Holy Spirit, whom the Father will send in my name, will teach you all things and will remind you of everything I have said to you."*
>
> —*John 14:26 NIV*

MADE IN HIS IMAGE

We are all made in the image of God. The word *image* is defined as "a reflection, or a resemblance of." When God looks at you, He sees Himself; you are the apple of His eye. The word *make*—as in your being "made" in His image—means "to bring into being by shaping, altering, or combining materials." You have been made with God-material! After God created man long ago in the Garden of Eden, He blessed them; to *bless* means "to make worthy of adoration, respect, or devotion." You are the object of God's affection! You are not here by default; God brought you here for a specific purpose.

> *I praise you because I am fearfully and wonderfully made; your works are wonderful, I know that full well. My frame was not hidden from you when I was made in the secret place, when I was woven together in the depths of the earth. Your eyes saw my unformed body; all the days ordained for me were written in your book before one of them came to be.*
>
> *—Psalm 139:14–16* NIV

According to this verse, God spent months anticipating your arrival on earth! He watched you while you were in your mother's womb being "woven together," and He has never stopped watching over you ever since. Every single moment of your life has already been laid out before you. God is not worried about your future, because He knows that He is the One who is completing the good work in you: "Being confident of this very thing, that he which hath begun a good work in you will perform it until the day of Christ" (Philippians 1:6 KJV).

God Himself is the One responsible for bringing you to your destination; all He requires is that you follow His leading. God created you, and He knows exactly what gifts He has placed within you. He will not require something of you if He had not already placed the ability within you to complete the task. Everything that you need has already been placed inside of you—albeit in seed form. You must reproduce after your own kind. If you were born to do one thing, do not try to reproduce after someone else's kind. Is there something that God has been specifically speaking to you about? Is He speaking to you about writing a book, or perhaps starting a new business or ministry?

The key to your prosperity and success is to follow God's master plan for your finances. You will prosper as you follow His plan because "it is he who gives you the ability to produce wealth" (Deuteronomy 8:18 NIV). He did not withhold His only Son from you, so we know that He will not withhold anything else from you, either. There is nothing more precious than Jesus! God has a strong desire to see you prosper, but He also does not want you to become covetous. Start believing in yourself because God believes in you —not based on your own talents. God considered you worthy enough to receive His very best gift—that of His only Son.

REFLECTION

1. What does it really mean to be blessed?

2. Do you believe that everything that you need has already been placed inside of you?

3. Is there something that God has been asking you to do?

4. What is the key to your prosperity?

5. Do you believe in your ability to succeed?

WHO ARE YOU? AND WHERE ARE YOU GOING?

In Genesis 16, we read the story of Hagar, who was originally an Egyptian slave. After ten years of waiting, Sarah eventually grew tired of the unfulfilled promise of a child. Ultimately, she did not believe that she would ever receive the child promised by the Lord, since she was advancing in age, so she asked Hagar to have a baby with her husband. As her slave, Hagar had no choice but to fulfill the demand of Sarah. Hagar was forced to have sexual relations with a man who did not love her, who only wanted to impregnate her. It is easy to sympathize with Hagar as we read her story, because she was faced with an emotionally taxing burden. Not only might she not be able to mother her only child, but she also had every reason to despise Sarah, her mistress. Abraham planned to have Sarah be the mother to the child that Hagar would carry inside of her for nine months. In addition to this, Sarah mistreated Hagar so terribly that she finally ran away from the abuse and ended up in the desert.

The angel of the Lord found Hagar—which means that he was looking for her. Hagar probably thought that she was all alone in the desert, but she did not know that God was looking for her. The angel asked her two very important questions, ones that we must all ask of ourselves: "Where have you come from? And where are you going?" The angel of the Lord spoke purpose to Hagar's life and told her the plans God had for her. Hagar had felt insignificant, and unseen by the world. She felt used by others, and she was in search of love and acceptance. Hagar was released into her purpose once she understood that the Lord "saw" her. He did not see her as a slave, but He saw her as a woman who needed love and acceptance. She learned that day that God sees everything we go through. She said, "You are the God who sees me," for she said, "I have now seen the One who sees me" (Genesis 16:13 NIV).

REFLECTION

1. Are you waiting on an unfilled promise?

2. Do you believe that you will receive your promise?

3. Have you been tempted to create your own plan apart from God's plan?

4. Where would you like to see yourself financially in five years?

5. Do you believe that God is looking for opportunities to bless you?

DON'T SIT ON YOUR PURPOSE

There are too many people of God who have been sidelined due to condemnation. Hear what the Word says: "Therefore, there is now no condemnation for those who are in Christ Jesus" (Romans 8:1 NIV). If the enemy can't stop you, he will try to sideline you through condemnation. Moses was sidelined for forty years. He knew in his heart that he had been called to be a deliverer. Unfortunately, he tried to fulfill that calling through anger, and he killed an Egyptian who had attacked a Hebrew.

Moses fled to Midian and found himself sitting by a well—and from there, he sat on his purpose. Moses spent forty years in voluntary exile because he decided to judge himself for murdering the Egyptian. Moses was probably racked with guilt throughout those years for killing that Egyptian. He likely repented countless times for committing such a seemingly unpardonable sin. *Midian* means "judgment," and he ran right into judgment instead of running toward the mercy of God. In Exodus 3, Moses had an encounter with God at the burning bush that forever changed him. When the angel of the Lord greeted Moses, he did not speak to him about his past; he only spoke to him about his future.

Whenever we have an encounter with God, He will reveal the greatness that is inside of us. God gave Moses a mission, not a sentence. Moses was a deliverer, and yet he could not deliver himself—he needed an encounter with God in order to free him from the prison of his past. His encounter with the angel of the Lord freed him from condemnation and released him into his purpose.

REFLECTION

1. What has been holding you back financially?

2. What is your purpose?

3. Are you sitting on your purpose?

4. What is God saying to you about your future?

5. Do you believe that God has set you free from all condemnation? (Study Romans 8:33-34)

LIFE CAN BE EXCITING

Do not spend your life waiting to live. Some people place their lives on hold until they feel they are finally in the ideal circumstances. Some people put their lives on hold until marriage, others until they lose weight. Don't waste time! Learn to live life to the fullest, regardless of what stage you are in. Jesus came so "that you may have life, and that you may have it more abundantly" (John 10:10). When God is on your side, you are a majority. You can do anything with God on your side. God placed you here for a purpose. Discover that purpose and then pursue it with all your heart.

Although that task sounds simple enough, it may require hours of prayer and reading the Word to find out your divine calling, because your prosperity is tied to your purpose. Many people are asking God for direction. They are asking God to reveal His purpose for their lives. Perhaps you have said, "God, I don't know what You have called me to be. I don't know what to do with my life." Are you willing to sit in God's presence long enough to discover your purpose? Are you willing to stay in His presence until you finally hear from Him? God does have a greater plan for you and a greater call on your life. God is calling you to rise to a higher level in Him. The Lord says, "My thoughts are not your thoughts, neither are your ways my ways" (Isaiah 55:8 NIV). God has not called you to live a "small" life. He has not called you to "think small." He has called you to live a big life, a life that is full of adventure, surprise, and amazing testimonies.

God does not want you to live a mundane life. He wants you to live each day with expectation, because you are anticipating what He will do and how He will do it. You can live a life of excitement; your life does not have to be boring! Life does not have to be predictable. When you study the life of Jesus, you will notice that each day in His life was different. One day He healed; another day He might have been rebuking demons; and yet another day He was feeding five thousand people. Each day of His life was different; He never experienced two days that were exactly alike. Instead He lived a life of adventure, one of passion and excitement. He impacted the lives of others because He lived His life in the anticipation of seeing His Father work through His life. He woke up each day with anticipation that the Father would do something, and His expectations were fulfilled.

Many of us are going through life in a routine manner. We go through life expecting only the mundane and the usual. We don't expect God to do anything out of the ordinary, and we don't expect anything different to happen. We tell ourselves that Monday, Tuesday, Wednesday, Thursday, and Friday will be the same as they were the week before. But the Word of God says, "You do not have because you do not ask God" (James 4:2 NIV). You have what you say, and because you are expecting every day to be the same, each day is therefore the same!

God has a greater plan for you. He has plans that you have not yet discovered. Life does not have to be boring, because He is not a boring God. Look up at the sky; look at the birds and the fish. He created so many different varieties of fish, with all different colors, shapes, and sizes. Some people think that serving God must be boring; they have no idea that serving God can be fun! God wants to take you on amazing faith adventures, but He requires that you have childlike faith before He can do so. When you have childlike faith, you can then believe God for the impossible.

REFLECTION

1. Have you been waiting to live life to the fullest?

2. Do you believe that you can do anything with God on your side?

3. Are you willing to pursue your purpose with all of your heart?

4. Are you willing to sit in God's presence long enough to discover your purpose?

5. Are you a big thinker?

3

KEEPING YOUR THOUGHTS UNDER CONTROL

Finally, brothers and sisters, whatever is true, whatever is noble, whatever is right, whatever is pure, whatever is lovely, whatever is admirable—if anything is excellent or praiseworthy—think about such things.

—Philippians 4:8 NIV

If we are to progress financially, we must learn how to control our thoughts. The only limitations you have are the ones that you place upon yourself. Wherever you are today, it is the result of the thoughts that you had yesterday; therefore, it is so important that you monitor what you are thinking about today! If you are ever discouraged, lonely, or simply feeling down, examine your thoughts to discover the source of the negativity. You are God-designed, and you were born to be a success. Financial prosperity can only occur as you prosper in your soul. Your financial account reflects your soul account. The Scriptures say: "Beloved, I wish above all things that thou mayest prosper and be in health, even as thy soul prospereth" (1 John 1:2 KJV). Before you can prosper financially, you must first learn to prosper in your soul, which consists of your mind, your will, and your emotions.

PRODUCTIVE THOUGHTS

"I know the thoughts that I think toward you," says the Lord, "thoughts of peace, and not of evil, to give you a future and a hope."

—*Jeremiah 29:11* NKJV

Spend time dwelling on productive thoughts, because thoughts always precede action. If you believe that you can never be successful, then you will never step out of your comfort zone in order to achieve success! You will never rise higher than the expectations you have of yourself. Never entertain thoughts of failure; instead counteract all negative thoughts with the things that God has said about you in His Word: You are more than a conqueror, and yes, you can do all things through Christ who strengthens you! Keep speaking the Word of God until the negative thoughts stop bombarding your mind.

There may be days when it is a continuous struggle to align your thinking with God's thoughts about you. Still, do not grow weary; the enemy is only trying to wear you down. We are encouraged to "resist the devil and he will flee" (James 4:7 NIV). You will never accomplish more than you believe is possible in your life. But you must know the Word of God in order to rein in your thoughts. Your thoughts should stay primarily on what the Word of God says about you. It is critical that you learn to control your thoughts. Here is an important question: Would you be at all embarrassed to allow me to spend a day reading your thoughts? We all have thoughts that are contrary to what we believe, but what sets believers apart from everyone is that we choose to do different things with our thoughts. Luke 2 states that our thoughts will be revealed (2:35). One of the ways that they are revealed is through our lifestyles.

REFLECTION

1. Are you a positive thinker?

2. What are your expectations concerning your finances?

3. What are some negative thoughts that are keeping you from prospering?

4. What do you believe is possible concerning your finances?

5. Write down some scriptures concerning your finances.

NO MORE CONFUSION

Many people are confused because they don't know God's plan for their lives. They don't know God's purpose because they have not spent enough time in God's presence. Their minds are cluttered, and they can't seem to focus. They don't know what direction in which they should go. They try to figure out the plan of God, to no avail. They repeatedly try to work out a plan, only to repeatedly fail. They are desperate to find out why success has so eluded them. They struggle because they can't seem to discover God's plan and purpose for their lives. We are told that "many are the plans in a person's heart, but it is the LORD's purpose that prevails" (Proverbs 19:21). If the Lord is not answering your cries, it is likely because you are following the wrong plan. Your plans must lead to God's purpose for your life. But from now on, you will have clarity of mind and clarity of thought as you follow His plans for you. You will begin to hear His voice more clearly, and your mind will function at a level that it has never functioned at before. You will become sharp in your thinking, so sharp that it becomes easy for you to formulate creative ideas and plans. You will begin to see what you have not been able to see before. Perhaps your thought processes have been confused. But now you will no longer be confused; you will begin to receive direction from the Lord.

REFLECTION

1. Are you clear about what God has called you to be?

2. What is keeping you from receiving clarity from the Lord?

3. What do you need to focus on?

4. What are some plans in your heart? Spend some time asking God to reveal to you if those desires are His plans.

5. Spend some time this week praying for creative ideas.

REPROGRAMMING YOUR MIND FOR ABUNDANCE

Our mind-set is typically one of the greatest obstacles to overcome on our journey to financial freedom. Poverty can, indeed, be a very difficult mind-set to overcome. It is possible to become so focused on our perceived lack that we lose any vision of abundance. When Moses led the Israelites out of Egypt, they could not let go of that Egypt mind-set, and they were never able to grasp a vision of the future. They could not embrace the future God had for them without first releasing their past. In a sense, they had selective memory: They remembered eating well in Egypt, but they somehow forgot the mistreatment they received there. If we are not careful ourselves, our minds can cause us to revert to our previous lifestyle of poverty.

Many lottery winners sabotage their own financial well-being, simply because of their inability to manage a new level of wealth. The numbers in their bank accounts might have changed, but the mind-set that had originally caused lack in their lives remained exactly the same. These lottery winners often encounter difficulties that are impossible for them to overcome, due to their sudden wealth; some of them subconsciously consider that they might be happier if they just got rid of their wealth. They begin to view the money, not as a source of joy, but as a source of discontentment. Sudden wealth has caused many people to lose relationships. You will discover who your true friends are when you refuse to lend them money. You must renew your mind-set concerning God's master plan for your finances. Wrong thinking could cause you to camp in the land of "just enough." The land of "just enough" is where your bills are paid but there is no extra money left over to accomplish the plan of God for your life.

REFLECTION

1. Do you have the right mind-set to prosper?

2. What can you do to change your mind-set?

3. Do you see abundance or do you see lack?

4. What will it take for you to leave the land of "just enough?"

5. Are there ways that you have been sabotaging your own financial prosperity?

OVERCOMING A POVERTY MENTALITY

I grew up surrounded by financial lack, and I developed a poverty mind-set because of my upbringing. When I was growing up, my family of four had to share a one-bedroom apartment. We all slept in the same bedroom, only separated from each other by a makeshift curtain. There was no financial "wiggle room" for any extras.

I struggled with a poverty mind-set as God began to increase me financially. One day, while in prayer, I saw a picture of a house flash before my eyes. I heard the Lord say *I am going to give you this house*. I proceeded to look online to locate the house that I had seen while I was in prayer, and I dealt with sticker shock once I found it and saw its price. How could I afford such house at such a young age? I reasoned that I did not need that house in order to validate me. I had trouble receiving God's blessings at that time, but by God's grace, I purchased the house only a few months later.

I thought that my biggest battle would be in the actual purchase of the house, but I soon found out that I was now living in a house that my mind-set could not handle. Each year I tried to sell the house, to no avail. I even tried setting the selling price far lower than my competitors. I am embarrassed to admit it now, but I actually attempted to sell that house for a few years. Each summer, I would list the house, only to later remove the listing in the fall. I finally discovered that my true motive for wanting to sell the house was that I had not stretched my thinking to the level of the house. I had received the house as an act of God's grace, and not because my faith was strong enough to receive it. Once I understood this reality, I began to pray that God would begin to stretch my thinking.

The Israelites never overcame their old mind-set, which was keeping them from entering their promised land. It should have been an eleven-day journey to the border of Canaan, and yet it took the Israelites forty years to get there. Most of the generation who had left Egypt never saw the promised land, simply because they could not let go of the past. Your life experiences have formed your core beliefs about money. Perhaps you grew up in extreme poverty, in which you were raised to believe that money is hard to make, or perhaps you grew up in a wealth of abundance, believing that money is easy to make. You must begin to prosper in your soul first, before you can prosper financially, so renew your mind concerning God's will for your finances.

Some people are struggling at their current financial level even though they are in a good place financially. They may find themselves in a financial position that they never imagined for themselves, and they do not feel worthy of God's blessing in this way. But they got to that level because of the blessing and favor of God. Their mind-sets are now working against them, trying to bring them down. You are worthy of financial abundance! God counted you worthy when He sent His Son to die for you on the cross. Why would God be willing to sacrifice His only Son for you, only to then withhold "unrighteous mammon" from you? (see Luke 16:9 KJV). Why would God be willing to pay the ultimate price for you, without then counting you worthy to receive anything more? You are worthy to break out of financial bondage! God paid the ultimate price for you because you are priceless in His sight.

REFLECTION

1. Did you grow up surrounded by abundance or by lack?

2. In what ways has your upbringing affected your mind-set about prosperity?

3. Has your mind-set limited your ability to prosper?

4. How can you stretch your thinking to a higher level of financial success?

5. Spend some time praying this week, asking God to stretch your thinking.

SEE BEYOND WHERE YOU ARE

Many people attempt to pray about their finances, but all they can see is the credit card debt, the mortgage payments, and the student loans that are due. They cannot see beyond their situation filled with debt. You must get out of the "debt mind-set," and stop seeing yourself as forever being in debt. Instead begin to see yourself prospering and writing big checks to other people, to other ministries. Begin to see yourself depositing big checks so that you can give to God's Kingdom. If necessary, write yourself a big check and then take a picture of it—to serve as a reminder of your financial forecast.

The Lord wants to change your financial level. No more debt! God did not borrow money when He created the earth. He did not borrow money when He created the sun. He did not borrow money when He created the oceans. So why do some people believe that they can only open a business by borrowing money to get started? God knows how to create without borrowing, and He can help you start a new business without borrowing the money. God did not free you from the bondage of sin only to deliver you into the bondage of financial debt. His Word tells us that the "borrower is slave to the lender."

REFLECTION

1. Can you see beyond where you now are financially?

2. Have you developed a "debtor's mind-set?"

3. Do you believe that God has creative financing ideas for you?

4. What does the Bible say about a borrower?

5. Do you feel overwhelmed by your debt? Pray for a strategy to be forever free from debt.

FACE YOUR GOLIATH

When David faced Goliath, the strongest men in the Israelite army stood by quaking with fear, but David had a different mind-set. He did not size up Goliath against his own size; he sized up Goliath against the size of his God. He concluded that Goliath was no match against his God. How do you react when you face your own financial Goliath? You may feel that your Goliath is the mountain of debt that is facing you. Your mountain of debt is no match for the size of your God. You can trust God to help you slay your own financial Goliath!

In 2 Kings, we read a story about a widow who was also facing a mountain of debt in her life. Her husband had died leaving her with many unpaid debts, and her creditors were so ruthless that they were planning to take her two sons to serve as slaves for the repayment of those debts. Seeing her plight, the Lord sent the prophet Elisha to help her out of her seemingly hopeless situation. When Elisha asked her, "How can I help you? Tell me, what do you have in your house?" the woman replied that she had nothing in her possession but a jar of oil (2 Kings 4:2 NIV). She was then instructed to borrow vessels so that she could sell the oil that would come from that one jar in order to pay off her debts: Elisha told her to "go borrow vessels from everywhere, from all your neighbors—empty vessels; do not gather just a few" (2 Kings 4:3).

The Lord is not limited in His methods. Elisha's advice might go against conventional wisdom; why would anyone ask a widow to borrow anything more when she is already head over heels in debt? But God has creative ways to deliver you from your mountain of debt. He gave this widow a lucrative oil business to help her pay off her debts, and she made enough profit to not only pay off her debt, but also to live off the rest. She went from crying about her financial failure to becoming a business mogul. The Lord is no respecter of persons, and He has many creative ways to prosper you. You can prosper financially! You are not limited by your bank account, the economy, your debts, or even your income. Are you open to receiving a creative idea from the Lord?

REFLECTION

1. Do you believe that God has enough money to bail you out of your current financial predicament?

2. How can you conquer your own financial Goliath?

3. Can you trust God to help you slay your own financial Goliath? Study the story of David and Goliath. (1 Samuel 17)

4. What are your personal resources and abilities?

5. Do you feel limited by your bank account?

4

THE WORDS OF YOUR MOUTH

The tongue also is a fire, a world of evil among the parts of the body. It corrupts the whole body, sets the whole course of one's life on fire, and is itself set on fire by hell.

—James 3:6 NIV

The words that come out of your mouth reveal what is truly in your heart. The Lord promised Moses, "I will be with your mouth, and teach you what you shall say" (Exodus 4:12). The Lord will never inspire you to say anything that would cause you to self-destruct; instead He inspires you to greatness. We are admonished in the book of Psalms to keep the Word of God continually on our lips. Your words are constantly creating your destiny. God said that the words that go out of His mouth will not return to Him void. You are made in the image of God; therefore, you must remember that the words that go out of your mouth will not return to you void. When God speaks, it happens; when you speak, it happens, too. Speaking the Word of God over your life will produce a harvest. The Word cannot return to God without producing the expected results.

One word of God has enough power to create whatever it is told to create. God creates with His word; you create with your words. Unfortunately, many of us spend our time saying the wrong things, thereby creating the wrong things in our lives. We speak out of frustration rather than choosing to speak on purpose. Those who understand the power of words actually learn to speak fewer words: "A person who talks too much gets into trouble. A wise person learns to be quiet" (Proverbs 10:19).

WORDS ARE POWERFUL

Your words are powerful, and you must say only what God says if you desire His results. Many people have destroyed their lives by the words of their mouths. The words of your mouth create what you eventually see with your physical eyes. When God said, "Let light be," it is still being. When you say, "God, I thank You that I am prosperous," those very words begin to create prosperity in your life. Your words begin to create the things that you declare over your life; therefore, be very careful of the words that come out of your mouth. Many people do not consider the creative process when they speak. They speak out of frustration, disappointment, or a lack of awareness of the power of their words. They fail to understand that when they speak, they are literally creating the very things that they spoke about.

You are creating the words that you speak. Because we were all taught to read by using the alphabet, we may think that our words are simply letters being spoken out into the atmosphere. But when you speak, your words are actually pictures that create things. When you speak the word *prosperity,* the picture of prosperity is created in your life. When you say the word health, the picture of health is created in your life.

REFLECTION

1. Do you believe that your words have power?

2. What have you been saying concerning your finances?

3. Do you need to repent of some negative words that you have spoken concerning your finances?

4. What are you creating with your words?

5. Do you have a clear picture of what you would like to create?

DO NOT CURSE YOUR FUTURE

Some people curse their own futures by constantly telling themselves that they are not capable: "I can't…I can't." Do not speak negatively about yourself. Some people repeatedly call themselves "dumb," "fat," or "poor," along with a list of other words that should not even be uttered. Only speak what you really believe in your heart. Do not say things out of frustration. Only speak what you want to have affirmed in your life. When you speak something, you are adding an "amen" to it; you are saying "so be it!" Do not curse what God has blessed, namely you! He has put you in a right position with Him, so do not create limitations in your life by restricting yourself with your words. You can find yourself bound by the words of your mouth.

We are reminded in the book of Proverbs that your words can restrict your progress: "You have been trapped by what you said, ensnared by the words of your mouth" (Proverbs 6:2 NIV). You can create a trap for yourself by speaking wrong things over your life. Tear down the walls that you have built with your negative words. Begin to speak only affirming words over yourself. Richard Bach once said, "Argue for your limitations, and sure enough, they are yours." Purpose in your heart not to transgress with your mouth.

Because you are a human being, watching your words does not guarantee that you will never say the wrong thing with your mouth. If you do find yourself saying the wrong thing, stop immediately and ask God for His forgiveness. Take time before you speak, so that your words will always agree with what you really believe. We have all spoken words that we later regretted. Whatever is in your heart will eventually come out of your mouth, so continually examine what is in your heart.

Anything spoken forth that is against your true beliefs is actually "filthy communication" (see Colossians 3:8 KJV). Have you ever said something to someone in anger without thinking? Do not be quick to speak. The direction of a horse can be determined by putting a small bit in his mouth. The direction of our lives is largely determined by the direction of our mouths. Where are you aiming your mouth? Are you aiming it toward success or failure? A great ship is directed by only a small helm. We are told in the book of James that although our tongue is a small member of our bodies, it alone can determine the course of our lives. Our tongues control the direction of our lives. You will create your future with your words. If you desire your life to go in a different direction, change the words that you have been speaking. Words accompanied by action will produce the desired effect in your life. Let everything in your life come into unity with your purpose.

REFLECTION

1. What are some negative words that you need to remove from your vocabulary?

2. Do you need to repent for some negative words that you have spoken?

3. What limitations and excuses have you placed upon yourself?

4. Are you aiming your words toward success?

5. Spend some time this week speaking affirming words over yourself and your future.

THE QUALITY OF YOUR QUESTIONS

In 1 Samuel 3 the importance of asking God the right questions is demonstrated. While David and his men were away in Achish, the Amalekites raided Ziklag. The entire town was destroyed by fire and the families of David and his men were taken captive. All of the men, including David, cried until they had no strength left to cry. But once David was done crying, he spent time contemplating his options, eventually determining that the best course of action was to pursue the kidnappers and rescue the captives. But before David took off on his rescue mission, he inquired of the Lord. He asked God two very specific questions: "Shall I pursue this raiding party?" and "Will I overtake them?" (1 Samuel 30:8 NIV). The Lord answered David, "Pursue them. You will certainly overtake them and succeed in the rescue" (1 Samuel 30:8 NIV).

David allowed himself a brief period of grieving, but then he took action. He did not allow himself to dwell in self-pity. David did not just ask for wisdom; he asked God two specific questions, to which he received two very specific answers. I truly believe that the quality of your questions determines the quality of your answers. When was the last time you asked God a specific question in prayer? Did you wait long enough to receive the answer from Him?

REFLECTION

1. What are some specific questions that you are asking of the Lord?

2. Are you willing to keep praying until you receive the answers?

3. What actions do you need to take this week that will begin the turn around in your finances?

4. Are you ready to overcome financial lack?

5. Spend some time this week thinking about a strategy for turning around your finances.

SHUT YOUR MOUTH

The angel of the Lord visited Zechariah to confirm that his prayer for a child was to be answered. The angel told him that his wife would give birth to a son named John (later to be John the Baptist). He further gave Zechariah instructions on how he was to raise his son. Zechariah did not believe what he was hearing. He asked the angel, "How can I be sure of this? I am an old man and my wife is well along in years" (Luke 1:18 NIV). The angel was shocked to hear Zechariah accusing him of lying about the promise. The angel answered, "I am Gabriel. I stand in the presence of God, and I have been sent to speak to you and to tell you this good news. And now you will be silent and not able to speak until the day this happens, because you did not believe my words, which will come true at their appointed time" (Luke 1:19–20 NIV).

Zechariah was left mute because his words were not in agreement with the plan of God. His wife may have stayed barren all those years because of the words of his own mouth. He could have possibly created his own barren situation by the words that he was speaking all that time. He might have continually expressed his doubts of ever having a child since he was advancing in age. But the angel shut his mouth so that he could not "miscarry" the promise of God.

Many of us have remained barren in our finances, and we have miscarried our abundance through the words of our mouths. Zechariah was not able to speak until the promised child had been delivered. We read in Proverbs 10 that "in the multitude of words sin is not lacking, but he who restrains his lips is wise" (verse 19).

It is better to just hold your tongue until you can use your words to create the right outcome.

I once experienced a serious betrayal from a friend. I began to continually complain to the Lord about how this friend had mistreated me; I kept rehearsing the story. I would share it with anyone who was willing to listen, and each time I shared the story, my emotions would get all riled up. I was stuck in a negative cycle, and I was starting to feel worn out over the whole experience. Finally, one day, out of desperation, I asked God for wisdom concerning the whole situation. As I prayed I heard Him say, *You must shut your mouth; stop talking about it.* From that moment on, I made the commitment to let the offense go and I stopped rehashing the story. The words of my mouth had been keeping me from moving forward.

REFLECTION

1. Are you doubting the promises of God concerning prosperity?

2. Do you believe that God is faithful to His promises?

3. Is there something you should stop talking about all the time?

4. Are your words in agreement with God?

5. Do you need to apologize to someone for the words you have spoken?

WHERE ARE YOU STEERING YOUR LIFE?

The words of your mouth determine the direction that your life is headed. Your words are literally creating a path to your destination. The Scriptures state that "the tongue has the power of life and death" (see Proverbs 18:21). Many people have killed their own dreams by the words of their mouths. Your words determine your course, just as the rudder of a ship determines its course. You can almost always guess someone's financial future based on the words that they speak. Their words are either putting them on the road to financial freedom or on the road to financial bondage.

You can literally set up a financial trap by the words of your mouth. If in the past you have ever used your words to dig yourself into a financial hole, it is not too late to change your course. You can begin today to use your words to dig yourself back out of that financial pit. Your words may have gotten you in that predicament, but it will also be your words that will get you out!

REFLECTION

1. Have you miscarried your abundance through the words of your mouth?

2. Do you plan to use your words to dig yourself out of financial lack?

3. Do you find yourself complaining a lot about your bills?

4. Are you speaking the solution or the problem?

5. Are you ready to start praising God for your turnaround?

5

REMOVING THE LIMITS

Jabez cried out to the God of Israel, "Oh, that you would bless me and enlarge my territory! Let your hand be with me, and keep me from harm so that I will be free from pain." And God granted his request.

—1 Chronicles 4:10 NIV

Smith Wigglesworth once said, "There is nothing impossible with God. All the impossibility is with us when we measure God by the limitations of our unbelief." As children, we were free to dream and to explore the world without reservations, but as we grew older we allowed others to limit us. We so often allow the limitations of others to keep us from dreaming. Many of us have learned to merely accept the status quo, and we have become keenly aware of the impossibilities in our lives. But God is looking for some more dreamers like Joseph. He is looking for those who will refuse to give up despite the opposition in life. Choose to remove any limits in your way; take yourself out of the box of limitations. You serve a limitless God, and therefore you are limitless in your potential! However, this calls you to break out of your comfort zone. Moses had to move out of his comfort zone. We find Moses arguing with God's purpose for his life in the book of Exodus:

"Pardon your servant, Lord. I have never been eloquent, neither in the past nor since you have spoken to your servant.

I am slow of speech and tongue." The Lord said to him, "Who gave human beings their mouths? Who makes them deaf or mute? Who gives them sight or makes them blind? Is it not I, the Lord? Now go; I will help you speak and will teach you what to say."

—*Exodus 4:10–12* NIV

Moses told God that he was not a speaker, but God was not calling forth a speaker. He was calling forth a deliverer, and the speaking was secondary. He was not surprised by Moses' inability to speak; He already knew about that when He called him into his purpose. When Moses told God about his limits, God spoke to him about his abilities. He reminded Moses that He was the one who had created his mouth, and so He already knew what Moses could do. Moses had not been chosen for his speaking ability, but he had been chosen because God knew that he would be willing to be His voice to the Israelite people. He told Moses that He would teach him what to say. When you place limits on yourself, you will limit what God can do in your life.

REFLECTION

1. Are you willing to dream again?

2. How determined are you to stay the course in spite of all oppositions?

3. How have you been limiting yourself?

4. Have you been telling God that the vision He has given you is not possible?

5. What are some rewards that you could reap for following your dreams?

PUSH PAST THE DISCOMFORT

When you attempt to break out of your comfort zone, your mind and your emotions will likely challenge you every step of the way. It can be painful to push past your own limitations. But do not give up, for there is a reward waiting on the other side of your pain. Jesus experienced great agony when He was facing the cross, but He focused on the rewards instead of the pain that He had to endure.

You must also focus on the reward of pushing past your limits. I promise you that the reward will be greater than the pain. Do not allow your emotions to keep you from your destiny. Your emotions are temporary, but your destiny has an everlasting impact. We should not make any life-changing decisions based on our feelings, because emotions can cloud our judgment. Sometimes it's best to wait on a major decision until your emotions have been sorted out.

REFLECTION

1. Are you resting in the promises of God?

2. Do you believe that God will do His part?

3. Do you believe God can get you to the "promised land?"

4. Are you dedicating time to studying your area of expertise?

5. Who are some people that you could network with to help you prosper?

YOU ARE A GIANT

In the book of Numbers, Moses sent out some spies to explore the land of Canaan. God had given them the land, but they still had to go out and possess it. All they needed to do was to study the land and come up with a strategy to conquer it. Moses gave them a list of what to research:

> *See what the land is like and whether the people who live there are strong or weak, few or many. What kind of land do they live in? Is it good or bad? What kind of towns do they live in? Are they unwalled or fortified? How is the soil? Is it fertile of poor? Are there trees on it or not?*
>
> —*Numbers 13:18–20* NIV

The Israelite spies were overcome with fear once they saw the "giants." Their leaders forgot who they were, and they focused on what they saw instead of what God had said. He had said, "Send some men to explore the land of Canaan, which I am giving to the Israelites" (Numbers 15:2 NIV). Caleb, however, had a conquering spirit, and he was not intimidated by the giants. He said, "We should go up and take possession of the land, for we can certainly do it" (Numbers 15:33 NIV).

The other leaders were filled with fear rather than faith. In contradiction to Caleb, they reported, "We seemed like grasshoppers in our own eyes, and we looked the same to them." How did these leaders know that the Canaanites saw them as grasshoppers? Grasshoppers are interesting creatures; these insects do not cause much damage when they are found alone, but a swarm of grasshoppers can wreak havoc in a place. Locusts are a group of grasshoppers that migrates in a swarm. One grasshopper alone cannot cause much trouble. But the shy grasshopper can turn into a giant monster when gathered in a group. A swarm of locusts can easily cover over four hundred square miles! Locust swarms are still feared to this day, because they can include billions of hungry grasshoppers. These insects will eat everything in sight, thereby devastating an area.

The Israelite leaders did not understand the concept that one grasshopper could group together with other grasshoppers to become a teeming swarm of locusts and take on bigger territory. These leaders focused on themselves instead of focusing on God's ability to deliver them. They reasoned that they themselves could not take on the giants, but they failed to realize that their strength lay in their numbers. Although each one felt small in his own eyes, together they could have accomplished the impossible. They were more than capable of taking the territory because the Lord had already given them the land.

REFLECTION

1. How can you possess your land?

2. How can you study your land?

3. Why were the Israelite leaders filled with fear?

4. Are you willing to take God at His word?

5. What will be your focus?

UNFAMILIAR TERRITORY

Perhaps you have felt as if you have been walking on a tightrope and you are afraid of falling. You are asking, *God, am I going to fall?* You may feel as if you are walking on a balance beam, and you may be wondering whether God will catch you if you tip off of it. You must trust Him as you are heading into new territory. Perhaps you have been doubting whether you will be able to make it to the other side, but He says to you that yes, you will, indeed, make it to the other side.

God will open the right doors for you at the right time. God does not leave anything half-finished. We must look "unto Jesus the author and finisher of our faith" (Hebrews 12:2 KJV). He is the same God who, in the book of Genesis, "By the seventh day finished all the work he had been doing." He never starts anything that He does not intend to finish. So put your hand in God's hand and walk across the balance beam with Him, simply by putting one foot in front of the other. You must be willing to say, *God, I don't know where I am going, but I am willing to follow You.*

God has promised you in His Word that "He shall give His angels charge over you, to keep you in all your ways. In their hands they shall bear you up, lest you dash your foot against a stone" (Psalm 91:11–12 NKJV). Why would you ever think that the Lord would let you fall when He is asking you to walk with Him? You will not stumble nor fall, because He will carry you when you are unable to walk. Perhaps you have been afraid to look down. Don't look down; instead look up to Jesus, for when you look down you will notice the circumstances around you. As you look down, you will hear what others are saying concerning you. As you look down, you will see the obstacles appearing bigger than they really are. But when you look up, the obstacles will seem smaller, and everything will be possible to you. You will see your circumstances changing, and you will see how God is coming through for you. Do not worry; God will bring you all the resources that you need in order to fulfill His purpose for you.

REFLECTION

1. Are you afraid of failing?

2. Can God fail?

3. What are some obstacles that are standing in your way? Speak to those obstacles.

4. Who do you need to rely on to bring all of the resources that you need?

5. Spend some time this week praying for open doors of opportunity.

BELIEVE GOD FOR THE IMPOSSIBLE

Are you believing God for the fulfillment of a seemingly impossible dream? Many times it is hard for others to believe in your dreams because they don't have your vision. They can't see what you see, because you are seeing your dream through the eyes of faith. Not everyone will see what you see.

Many people laughed at Venus and Serena Williams's father when he shared his dream of raising two world-class tennis champions. He spent many hours imagining his dream. He conceived of this dream before his children were even born. It is amazing to think that his daughters were actually born to fulfill this purpose. Their father even took the time to type out a seventy-five-page plan of how he would accomplish this dream.

It does not matter how impossible your dream may seem, God majors in the impossible. Jesus said, "With man this is impossible, but with God all things are possible" (Matthew 19:26 NIV). Do not give up on your dreams, even if you have spent years waiting on their fulfillment. Don't be afraid: It took Abraham twenty-five years before he received his promised son. Abraham's faith was tested throughout all of those years, but because he persevered, he received the promise.

The book of Hebrews shares how Sarah received this very promised child: "Through faith also Sara herself received strength to conceive seed, and was delivered of a child when she was past age, because she judged him faithful who had promised" (Hebrews 11:11 KJV). Sarah received the promised child because she had faith; she dared to believe in the God who majors in changing impossible situations.

REFLECTION

1. Are you willing to follow God's instructions?

2. Are you expecting others to be equally excited about your vision?

3. Do you believe that God has a dream for you?

4. How long have you been waiting on your promise?

5. Do you believe it is too late for you to receive your promise?

WHAT DO YOU SEE?

At what are you focusing? Are you spending your time looking at the numbers in your bank account? God took Abraham outside, and He taught him to focus on the stars. He said, "I will make your descendants as numerous as the stars in the sky" (Genesis 26:4 NIV). God gave Abraham a mental picture so that he could envision his future. He showed him the stars, and then told Abraham, "Look up at the sky and count the stars—if indeed you can count them... So shall your offspring be" (Genesis 15:5 NIV).

God sometimes gives us short, bite-sized "commercials" of what our future will look like. We must choose to believe these previews when they come. Do you ever see yourself doing something that seems impossible? Your territory will never go beyond what you can see. The stars were a representation of the number of descendants that would come from Abraham's lineage. Certainly he had to make some sacrifices to fulfill this purpose; not all of his family members could go with him to the land the Lord had shown to him and so he had to leave those persons behind. You will also have to make some sacrifices in the fulfillment of your purpose; some things will have to be left behind.

God spent years speaking to Abraham about his purpose before he could truly believe in it. What are you using as a focal point to remind you of your dreams? Perhaps you need to keep looking at a picture of that car; or maybe you need to envision the house the Lord has for you. Are you believing for a child? When I was believing God to have a daughter, I kept a pair of little pink sandals to serve as my focal point. Each day I would look at those sandals and believe that one day my very own daughter would fill them with her feet. And later, when I went into labor to bring her into this world, I made sure to take those sandals with me. I put the sandals on my daughter's feet shortly after delivering my promised baby!

I also learned the importance of having a clear vision when I redecorated my family room. For ten years, I had dreamed about redecorating this room. Each year I would complain that the room did not feel inviting to me. I talked to others about my dissatisfaction with the room. Although I spent all of those years complaining about the room, I never took the time to write down a plan to change it. Finally, during the tenth year, I got tired of complaining about the problem and decided to do something about it. I sat down and wrote out a concrete plan to redecorate the family room. And within two weeks of writing down the plan, the room was fully redecorated to my satisfaction. I could not have done anything about changing the family room until I had a clear vision of the completed task. But once I had a clear vision, all of the resources came in alignment to fulfill my vision. I purchased all the supplies in one week at bargain prices. This experience taught me that nothing will ever change—unless I act. All of us will continue to struggle financially until we receive a clear vision for our finances. But the resources will come once we receive that clear vision. We must receive God's master plan for our finances!

REFLECTION

1. What do you see when you close your eyes and dream about your future?

2. What are you willing to sacrifice to accomplish your goals?

3. What are you using as a focal point to remind you of your promise?

4. Have you take the time to formulate a financial plan?

5. Are you ready to step out on faith?

6

DISCIPLINING YOURSELF

But I keep under my body, and bring it into subjection: lest that by any means, when I have preached to others, I myself should be a castaway.

—1 Corinthians 9:27 KJV

You must be willing to apply self-discipline in order to attain any level of success. You must acquire certain habits on the road to success. A *habit* is "an acquired pattern of conduct that has become almost instinctive because of recurrent actions." You must be willing to unlearn the habits that are hindering you. Cultivate your productive habits, and get rid of the habits that are hindering your progress.

I used to be a very undisciplined person, especially in my eating habits. I once developed a very strong affinity for eating brownies, and these brownies caused me to experience increase in the wrong area of my life. I finally determined that I would not allow brownies to rob me of my destiny, but I also knew that I did not have the willpower to quit eating them on my own. Each day, I would ask God to deliver me from my strong desire for sugar and chocolate. And I would be eating brownies while thanking God that I was freed from sugar and chocolate! Finally, one day my taste for sugar was completely gone, and when I tried to eat brownies, I discovered that they did not bring the same level of satisfaction as they had before. I was finally freed from my addiction to sugar and chocolate, and I lost ten pounds in two weeks' time!

Jesus had certain habits that helped Him to succeed in His life here on the earth. He had a habit of going to the synagogue to read the Word of God. He also practiced the discipline of fasting. He had a habit of withdrawing from the crowds to pray alone. When we fail to stay in the presence of God, we end up feeling empty and worn out. We must continually stay in His presence so that we can have something to give to other people. When you do not take time to fill yourself up with His Word and His presence, you will become depleted and you will not have much left over to give. We should strive to continually read God's Word. It is the Word of God that washes us and cleanses us from disappointment, discouragement, and sin.

The apostle Paul taught on the importance of discipline when he said, "I discipline my body and bring it into subjection, lest, when I have preached to others, I myself should become disqualified" (1 Corinthians 9:27 NKJV). We must develop positive habits that lead us to success. We must cultivate habits of prayer, self-control, and maintaining a steadfast focus on the Lord. The easiest way to break a habit is to start a new one. If you have had a bad habit of gossiping about others, don't become overwhelmed in the attempt to stop. Instead, focus on disciplining yourself to only speak good things about others.

DO NOT REJECT KNOWLEDGE

Most of us are not farmers because we now live in the Information Age. So how can we "labor" in this time in which we live? One way is through study. God's Word tells us that we "are destroyed for lack of knowledge. Because you have rejected knowledge, I also will reject you from being priest for Me; Because you have forgotten the law of your God, I also will forget your children" (Hosea 4:6 NKJV). There are several verses in Proverbs that emphasize the importance of such knowledge. God has provided several resources with which we can destroy our ignorance. It is knowledge that will cause you to succeed in this world.

We must acquire all types of knowledge—biblical as well as natural knowledge. We must be willing to learn the principles for the successful management of our personal finances. We should also be serious students of the Word of God. God instructed Joshua to "keep this Book of the Law always on your lips; meditate on it day and night, so that you may be careful to do everything written in it. Then you will be prosperous and successful" (Joshua 1:8 NIV).

We must also learn this world's system so that we can understand the best ways in which to operate in it. There are certain things that you must know before starting any new endeavor, whether you are starting a new business, writing a book, or starting a ministry. As we consistently practice the disciplines of the Christian faith, we can make our way prosperous. Our main goal in life must be to please the heavenly Father, but as we please Him, He leads us in the paths of righteousness, freedom, peace, and prosperity.

REFLECTION

1. How can you labor in your field?

2. What is one thing that has destroyed many people?

3. What knowledge do you need to acquire to succeed in your field?

4. Do you understand the principles of personal finance?

5. What is your main goal in life?

THE POWER OF FOCUS

I have found it extremely hard at times to stay focused on my vision. I have read several biographies of individuals who have gone on to accomplish great things, and the common thread among them seems to be their ability to stay focused on their vision. Jesus is the epitome of what it means to stay focused on a vision. He was so clear in His mission when He said, "For I did not come to judge the world, but to save the world" (John 12:47 NIV). Jesus lived His life completely focused on the mission of saving the world. He did not allow Himself to be distracted by anything that did not directly contribute to His purpose. Instead He spent each day working toward fulfilling the purpose the Father had made known to Him.

If you were to examine a day in the life of Jesus, you would likely notice that His schedule showed that of a man on a mission. His daily schedule always brought Him closer to fulfilling His purpose. And His purpose compelled Him to rise early in the morning. Each day, He went to a secluded place to pray, and then He spent the rest of his day preaching, teaching, and healing others. You, too, must remain focused on your goal, because others will try to steer you away from your vision.

An attempt was made to lure Jesus away from His mission, when "after the people saw the miraculous sign that Jesus did, they began to say, 'Surely this is the Prophet who is to come into the world.' Jesus, knowing that they intended to come and make him king by force, withdrew again to a mountain by himself" (John 6:14–15 NIV). He had to quickly get alone with God to recommit Himself to His purpose. We, too, should continually spend time alone with God in order to gain a clarity of His vision for us, lest we be derailed from our purpose. Evangelist Billy Graham was nearly distracted from his life's purpose when he was asked to run for president. But he answered, "God has called me to preach, and I do not intend to do anything else as long as I live."

The apostle Paul is another example of someone who was extremely focused on his God-given vision. Paul declared that he was called "to be a minister of Christ Jesus to the Gentiles" (Romans 15:16 NIV). Everything Paul did in his life supported this mission of preaching the Gospel to the Gentiles. Paul's extreme focus on his life's purpose enabled him to write two-thirds of the New Testament. In it Paul wrote these words: "No one serving as a soldier gets entangled in civilian affairs, but rather tries to please his commanding officer" (2 Timothy 2:4 NIV). You will be tempted to lose focus whenever you are faced with opposition. First Corinthians 11 describes some of the hardships that Paul had to overcome in order to accomplish his life's mission of preaching the Gospel to the Gentiles. He was beaten and shipwrecked. He faced many challenges, and yet he never gave up. What are you willing to endure to accomplish your dreams?

REFLECTION

1. How can you stay focused on your goals?

2. What distractions do you need to remove from your life?

3. How are you spending your time each day?

4. Does your daily schedule reflect your mission in life?

5. What are you willing to endure to accomplish your dreams?

LEARN FROM THE BEST

Studying other individuals who have experienced success in their fields can inspire us in our own journeys. As human beings, we all have flaws. We can learn from those who have achieved success in a particular field, even if such individuals are imperfect. One such individual who maintained extreme focus on his vision was Arnold Schwarzenegger. He might not have led a perfect life, but he can serve as an example of what it means to stay focused on your dreams. We are each a work in progress.

As a young boy, he developed the dream of becoming a bodybuilder. His desire was to emulate his hero, Reg Parc. Arnold's obsession with his dream compelled him to train five hours a day, seven days a week. As he read more about his hero, he discovered a blueprint to follow. From that time on, it did not matter how hard he had to work because he had a purpose. He smiled throughout the hard and laborious work, because he knew that every weight he lifted was bringing him one step closer to the goal of becoming Mr. Universe. When he was lifting weights, he treated the exercise as if he was lifting his newly won trophies. He pictured people celebrating his success in winning the Mr. Universe title.

Arnold was once asked whether he found it hard to eat only healthy food in order to maintain his physical shape, but he answered that he had "always been hungrier for something else." What are you hungry to accomplish? You must decide what it is that you really want. You must have a clear vision. You must decide the price that you are willing to pay in order to accomplish your vision. Select a role model in the field that you are desiring to master. Visualize a clear picture of yourself cultivating what it is you really want. Study your role model; study every move that this example has made. Find out everything you can about your role model. He or she will be the example that you will try to emulate. The more you focus on this image, the more you will see that it is real and possible for you to accomplish the very same vision in your own life. When you learn about the path that someone else has taken, it will make the idea of your own success become more concrete in your mind. Paul said, "Follow my example, as I follow the example of Christ" (1 Corinthians 11:1 NIV).

REFLECTION

1. Who are your role models?

2. Are you following a proven blueprint in your career field?

3. Are you willing to endure the hard work to accomplish your dreams?

4. Who are some people that you need to study?

5. Do you have a clear picture of what you would like to accomplish?

PUT GOD FIRST

Some people have failed to prosper because they believe that it is possible to trick the Lord. The Scripture say, "Seek ye first the kingdom of God, and his righteousness; and all these things shall be added unto you" (Matthew 6:33 KJV). Unfortunately, many people are still trying to seek first the things of the world, and then they expect God to be added to those things later. The Scriptures tell us to prioritize the Lord first; we are to seek God first and then everything else will be added unto us.

As you seek God first, the things that others are striving for, desiring, craving, and seeking will be added to you—effortlessly. You must first seek God with all your heart. You must be willing to make Him the number-one priority in your life. You must desire God's presence more than you desire your financial freedom. You must desire Him more than you desire any financial breakthrough. You must desire His presence more than you want to be prosperous. You must yearn to spend time in His presence, and as you seek Him, you will then get everything that belongs to Him.

We can't trick God because He knows our hearts—including all of our desires. He knows if He is truly the desire of your heart, or whether you are just pretending because you want Him to give you the things that you really desire. Many people are saying, "God, You are the desire of my heart," but is He really the desire of *your* heart? How much time are you spending in His presence in relation to how much time you are spending to gain other things in your life?

REFLECTION

1. Do you desire God's presence more than you desire financial freedom?

2. What is the number-one priority in your life?

3. Are you willing to persevere in the presence of the Lord even when you don't see immediate results?

4. How much time do you spend each day seeking God?

5. Faith requires you to act before you ever see the manifestation take place in your life. How can you act on your faith this week?

YOUR PROSPERITY PLAN

Alan Lakein once said, "Failing to plan is planning to fail." Successful organizations spend time in strategic planning. Strategic planning involves an organization's process of defining its strategy or its direction. It involves making decisions on how to allocate its limited resources. Many times, our dreams are delayed because we have not taken the time needed to plan. Your vision will become more clear as you invest the necessary time in the planning process. Suppose you decided to go on a cross-country road trip and yet you failed to plan your route. You may eventually get to your destination, but it will certainly take you longer because you failed to plan the most efficient route for your trip.

The same principle of planning applies to the pursuit of your dreams. If you fail to plan the specific steps you need to take to get to your destination, you may find yourself wandering in the desert for several years. The book of Proverbs admonishes all of us to "commit to the LORD whatever you do, and he will establish your plans" (Proverbs 16:3 NIV). How can God establish any plans if you have not taken the time to formulate anything? The Word gives us this blessing: "May he give you the desire of your heart and make all your plans succeed" (Psalm 20.4 NIV). But how can God prosper plans that do not exist? Again, in Proverbs we read, "In their hearts humans plan their course, but the LORD establishes their steps" (16:9 NIV). We are responsible for planning our course and the Lord will establish our steps. We must not be too busy to plan our course.

In Jeremiah, we read that the Lord is Himself a planner: "'For I know the plans I have for you,' declares the LORD, 'plans to prosper you and not to harm you, plans to give you hope and a future'" (29:11 NIV). Spend time dreaming, and then write out a detailed plan of how to get to your destination. Seek resources that will help you to accomplish your goals.

REFLECTION

1. How much time are you investing each week in the planning process?

2. What are some specific steps you need to take to get to your destination?

3. Are you willing to pursue your vision until you reach a level of success in that area?

4. What skill do you need to perfect?

5. Who is responsible for planning your course?

7

DO YOU SEE CLEARLY?

> *Suppose one of you wants to build a tower. Won't you first sit down and estimate the cost to see if you have enough money to complete it?*
>
> —*Luke 14:28* NIV

You should always assess your ability to finish any new endeavor before you start it, you must count the cost. There is a price to pay for success and few are willing to pay it. There are certain endeavors that require more commitment than others. One of the most discouraging things in life is to start something that you are not able to complete. A small real estate developer once had the dream of building a premier property near our local mall. His dream was to build a fifteen-story condominium and hotel.

Unfortunately, shortly after this developer began construction, he ran out of money. The developer owed sixty-six million dollars to his creditors, and he was forced to abandon the project. This developer has become notorious in our town for so many unfinished projects. His reputation became tarnished because he failed to count the cost of his plans. One councilman noted, "Everything that could go wrong on a property seemingly has gone wrong with this property." And for the next ten years, that property sat there with just a shell of a building constructed upon it, an eyesore in a prime location of the city. Years of litigation passed before the property finally was purchased by a new developer. The developer that purchased the property spent one year conducting diligent research before eventually purchasing it—counting the costs—and the new owners came to the table with sixty-six billion dollars in assets. The city council made sure that the new owners would have sufficient funds to complete the project.

Have you counted the costs? Are you willing to pay the price to fulfill your purpose? What is the one dream that you would be pursuing if you knew that you were guaranteed to succeed? You must be willing to use what you currently have in your hands. Be grateful, and do not despise small beginnings. Epicurus once said, "Do not spoil what you have by desiring what you have not; but remember that what you now have was once among the things only hoped for."

TALENT ACCORDING TO YOUR ABILITY

Many of us have been crying out to God about our financial situations, not realizing that God has already equipped us with the resources we need to succeed. God has given us talents and dreams to enable us to excel in our chosen fields. In the story of the parable of the talents, the master gave each man a talent, each according to his ability. He handed off his goods to three individuals: To one servant he gave five talents; to another he gave two; and to another he gave one talent according to his ability. When the master returned, he found out that two of his servants had doubled his assets, but the servant with the one talent had hidden it because he was afraid. The master was very pleased with the two servants who had doubled his money. He said to each servant, "Well done, good and faithful servant; you were faithful over a few things, I will make you ruler over many things. Enter into the joy of your lord" (Matthew 25:21 NKJV).

The one servant who had hidden his master's talent was cast into outer darkness, because he was found to be unprofitable by his master. He was despised because he did not use the ability that he had been given. The master had given him one talent, because that is what he was capable of handling. But instead of using his talent, he allowed fear to control his life, and thus he was not only unprofitable to himself, but he was also unprofitable to his master.

God expects you to use your abilities efficiently. Are you using your time to increase—spiritually, naturally, and financially? What do you spend most of your time doing? What you do today will determine your tomorrow. You should spend most of your time doing things that lead you toward your greater purpose.

REFLECTION

1. What are your talents?

2. How have you been utilizing your talents?

3. Have you allowed fear to control some areas of your life?

4. Do you consider yourself profitable?

5. Are you using your time efficiently?

MINE YOUR OWN FIELD

A minister by the name of Russell Conwell once gave a talk entitled "Acres of Diamonds," in which he illustrated how we so often underestimate the value of what we have. An old farmer once decided to sell his farm and go out in search of diamonds. He heard that diamonds had been discovered in Africa. He searched for many years, but he found no diamond until he had spent all of his money. The old farmer then threw himself into the ocean and drowned. One day the new owner of the property discovered a strange stone. When a merchant was passing by, the new farmer showed him the stone that he had found. It turned out that the entire farm was covered in acres of diamonds. The old farmer had gone out in search of something that he had possessed all along. You are God's diamond, and you are currently being polished. Diamonds are formed by great pressure, so if you are experiencing some of this pressure, relax! God is simply working on His masterpiece.

You have within you everything that you will ever need, and God has given you all spiritual blessings. Do not look elsewhere for treasure when it is lying right within you. To succeed in life, you must have a clear vision of what you would like to accomplish. What do you love to do? What do you spend your spare time doing? What comes the most naturally to you? Count your assets: What are your gifts? How much money do you have? How much time do you have? Evaluate your total assets in order to determine your starting point. It doesn't matter how little the amount, God can make up the difference as you go along.

We have been told not to compare ourselves with others. The Scriptures say that we are foolish when we do this. You can get discouraged when you compare your place in life to that of someone else's. When a 400-meter race takes place, the runners are given a staggered start so that they each run the exact same distance. We are all running the same distance in order to get to the purpose of God for our lives, but we must stay in our own lanes to get to the destination. We must remain focused lest we drift off into another runner's lane. We must run our own race without worrying about anyone else's. We are not chasing anyone else; instead we are chasing our own purpose.

Do not be concerned about is happening in someone else's life. You are not in competition with others, only with time. God has made you to be unique from everyone else. He did not create anyone else exactly like you. You are here because the world needs you and you can contribute something to the world that no else has been given. Theodore Roosevelt once said, "Do what you can, with what you have, right where you are." If you are not a five-talent person, then do the best you can with the one talent you have in your hands.

REFLECTION

1. Have you been underestimating the value of your abilities and resources?

2. How do you handle pressure?

3. Do you believe that you have what it takes to be successful?

4. How can you stop comparing yourself to others?

5. How can you take the first steps to financial success with your talents and abilities?

HARD WORK LEADS TO PROFIT

For years, I had a dream of becoming a writer. I spent many of those years dreaming without making much real progress. I kept making excuses and reasoned that I lacked the time because I was a mother and a wife. After years of frustration, however, I finally realized that it was up to me to fulfill my dream. I came to terms with the fact that I would never have all of the perfect ingredients completely ready that would allow me to fulfill this purpose. And so I made up my mind that I would no longer make any excuses. At that point I was finally able to fulfill my dream—once I wrote out a concrete plan for accomplishing it.

It took a tremendous investment of time and prayers to birth this book. I spent hours writing, sometimes getting up as early as three thirty in the morning. Some days I would write twelve hours a day. I also spent days, and sometimes nights, in prayer, asking God for inspiration for this book. It will take hard work to fulfill our purpose. The book of Proverbs tells us that, "All hard work brings a profit, but mere talk leads only to poverty" (Proverbs 14:23 NIV).

REFLECTION

1. What are the excuses that you tell yourself?

2. When do you plan to act to fulfill your dreams?

3. Are you ready to put all excuses aside?

4. Are you willing to invest in your dream?

5. How hard are you willing to work?

CLARITY IN YOUR VISION

Some people give up too easily. They quit before they receive the full details of the plan of God for their lives. They miss some key pieces to the puzzle, and yet they go ahead and run off, attempting to fill in the missing pieces. They try to complete the picture while lacking clarity in their vision. *Clarity* means "clearness as to understanding; freedom from ambiguity; sharpness of image or sound." Every person must stay in God's presence long enough until the picture for their lives becomes clear. They must stay there until every missing piece is put in place, and then they will be able to complete the picture. And once the picture is completed, they will be able to see it come to pass.

Many people believe that we actually think in words, but the truth is that human beings tend to think in pictures, because we are creators—just like God. He is the God "who sees the end from the beginning." We must have a clear vision before it can come to pass. Perhaps you have tried to picture your future, but you have not been able to pick up the right signal.

A television decodes electronic signals to project an image onto its screen, but there are times when the signal is interrupted. An interference occurs when an unwanted radio frequency signal disrupts your television, causing the image to be grainy. Perhaps you have experienced this type of interference when receiving a clear vision from the Lord for your life. You may have spent time praying, asking God for a clear plan, but you have not been able to receive any clear instructions. You may have asked God for a preview of your future, but each time you begin to receive this vision, you encounter interference and the picture is cut off. You may have given up because of this interference, walking away from the pursuit of the dream. Daniel did not walk away when he experienced this kind of interference; instead he pressed through, he pressed on, he stayed on his knees, and he fasted. He continued to seek the Lord until he received a direct signal and his picture was clear.

The Scriptures promise us that God has a great plan for each of us: "What no eye has seen, what no ear has heard, and what no human mind has conceived—the things God has prepared for those who love him" (1 Corinthians 2:9 NIV). Your eyes can see the plan of God, and your ears can hear what He has planned for you. Are you willing to stay long enough in His presence to be able to see what others have not seen, to be able to hear what others have not heard? Will you act like the majority of human beings on this planet and just give up? You must persevere in His presence until you receive His plan and you have been given the whole picture.

Perhaps you have been in a hurry to move forward in the plan of God, and you have not been willing to sit at His feet long enough to receive your instructions. You don't have to rush to accomplish the plan of God. He is the God of acceleration, and He can divinely speed up your process if that is needed. He never gets behind schedule, and He never gets ahead of His own schedule, either; He is an on-time God. He does everything in season, and He does not do anything out of season. He does everything according to His timetable, not according to our schedules.

Perhaps you are always rushing through life. Many people have destroyed their bodies in this accelerated process, because they are always in a hurry. Perhaps you have taken on too many responsibilities because you have felt that it was your job to bring about your own success. I encourage you to stop worrying, and to decide that you will no longer be in a hurry to get to your destination. Follow God's timetable; it is stress-free!

REFLECTION

1. Do you have a tendency to give up easily?

2. Are you able to see the end from the beginning?

3. Are you willing to wait patiently?

4. Do you believe that God can accelerate His plan for your life?

5. Are you willing to follow God's timetable?

DON'T BE A MULE

People are referred to as "sheep" in the Scriptures—not as mules. Mules are obstinate creatures that refuse to follow orders. God referred to us as "sheep," because we are expected to surrender our desires and follow His will for our lives. Sheep listen to their shepherd's voice and they follow. Mules are stubborn; they prefer to follow their own plans. Do not be a mule when the Lord has called you to be a sheep.

Some people are frustrated because the Lord seems to have taken His hands off their plans. But there cannot be two guides in your life: You can either lead your own life, or you can submit to the Lord's leading. He is a gentleman, and He will not fight you to control your life. He requires you to completely surrender to Him—voluntarily. When you submit to His plan, you enter a "sweet spot." Perhaps you have been experiencing a lot of challenges in your life, and you have felt like you were "going against the grain." It may have felt as if you were trying to swim against the tide, but get ready! You are about to ride the wave. You will enter a new period of grace to do what you have not yet been able to do. There will be a grace to accomplish what has seemed difficult. There is a grace coming that will allow you to reach territory that you have not been able to enter.

REFLECTION

1. Are you willing to surrender your plans to the Lord?

2. Do you know how to recognize the voice of God?

3. Are you following your plan or God's plan for your life?

4. Do you believe that God can give you the grace you to enter territory that you have not been able to enter?

5. How do you plan to tap into the grace of God to prosper?

8

WHAT WILL IT COST YOU?

"Suppose one of you wants to build a tower. Won't you first sit down and estimate the cost to see if you have enough money to complete it?"

—Luke 14:28 NIV

The famous oil tycoon H.L Hunt went bankrupt while raising cotton in Arkansas. He later went on to build a fortune of several billion dollars, becoming one of the world's richest men. He was once asked his formula for success. He said, "In America, you only need two things to be successful: first decide exactly what it is you want, and most people never accomplish that. Second, determine the price you're going to pay to get it, and then resolve to pay it." We each have our own definition of success. What is yours? You must answer that question: How can you reach an unknown target?

When you step into your purpose, God will provide the resources that are needed to fulfill that purpose. As you fulfill your divine purpose, the Lord will bring the necessary people and financial resources into your life. Our Father God had a mission, which was to see mankind restored to Himself. Although He knew that His mission would cost Him the ultimate price—His Son—He counted us worthy of that price. Jesus knew that His mission to save the world would cost Him the ultimate price—His life—and yet He chose to concentrate on the reward rather than on that price.

Although He suffered terribly on the cross, He considered the reward to be greater than the price. And we thank God today, because we would never have been redeemed had He counted the price as greater than the reward. The key to fulfilling your purpose is to follow the example of our Lord Jesus, by concentrating on the reward rather than on the cost. You should not ignore the cost, because how could you resolve to pay a price that you do not know? What will it cost to fulfill your potential? It will cost you both hard work and money.

PUSH PAST THE PAIN

Proverbs is full of wisdom on how to prosper financially. The Scriptures warn us that "whoever loves pleasure will become poor" (Proverbs 21:17 NIV). After you have evaluated the cost of success, ask yourself: What will it cost you if you do not fulfill your potential? The price that you pay in order to live with untapped potential is far greater than the price you would have had to pay to reach it. Once you resolve to pay the price, all of heaven backs you up. We would all like to hear one day, "Well done, good and faithful servant! You have been faithful with a few things; I will put you in charge of many things" (Matthew 25:21 NIV). You must be willing to push past the pain. It is not always smooth sailing when you are attempting to cross over an obstacle. Not all success necessarily comes easily.

When Jesus was facing the Garden of Gethsemane, He prayed, "Father, if you are willing, take this cup from me; yet not my will, but yours be done" (Luke 22:42 NIV). There are times during the pursuit of your purpose when you will be tempted to cry, and even be tempted to quit. If the road to success was a smooth one, then everyone would be on it. Few people experience the upper echelons of success because of their inability to bear discomfort. You must be willing to push past discomfort, because on the other side of that pain is your victory and the success that you desire.

Some people give up so easily; they expect to walk through life without having to face any obstacles. Unfortunately, however, there are times when you will have to deal with pressure in life. It is this pressure that refines you into pure gold. God supplies us with His grace to endure the pressure, even during the hard seasons of life. He will give you the grace to push past the difficulties and to walk on choppy waters. You must persevere to fulfill your purpose. You must not be quick to quit every time you encounter a difficulty.

The apostle Paul faced many challenges in his ministry. He felt weary of his opposition and he pleaded with the Lord to take away the pressure. But the Lord did not answer Paul's prayer in the way he expected; instead, the Lord promised him the grace to overcome the challenges. Paul shared this experience in the book of 2 Corinthians:

> *Therefore, in order to keep me from becoming conceited, I was given a thorn in my flesh, a messenger of Satan, to torment me. Three times I pleaded with the Lord to take it away from me. But he said to me, "My grace is sufficient for you, for my power is made perfect in weakness." Therefore I will boast all the more gladly about my weaknesses, so that Christ's power may rest on me. That is why, for Christ's*

sake, I delight in weaknesses, in insults, in hardships, in persecutions, in difficulties. For when I am weak, then I am strong.

—2 Corinthians 12:7–10 NIV

Many of us do not reach a high level of success because we have a low tolerance for pain. We expect everything to be easy. As soon as we encounter choppy waters, we are tempted to abandon ship. When we face opposition, we question whether we heard from God in the first place. Do not judge the Lord's leading based on the smoothness of the waters around you. It is possible that God has called you to walk on choppy waters before you experience smooth ones. Keep on walking past the obstacles; you *will* get to the other side.

REFLECTION

1. What will it cost you if you do not fulfill your potential?

2. Is the road to success always smooth?

3. Are you willing to push past all discomfort?

4. Do you believe that God will give you the grace to push past the difficulties?

5. Are you determined to keep walking past obstacles?

WHAT DOES IT TAKE TO PROSPER?

It takes determination to prosper. It takes a firm decision to follow God's plan. It takes a firm decision not to give up when things get hard. It takes a firm decision to go against the crowd when everyone else is doing one thing and you are being led by the Lord to do something different. It takes courage to go against what everyone else is saying and doing. Everyone else is following their own plans, spending money on whatever they desire without restraints. You must be willing to seek the Lord's guidance concerning your finances. You should consult Him on all of your major purchases. Be willing to ask Him whether it is His will for you to make that purchase at that particular moment.

Many people are concerned about how others may perceive them; they believe that they should follow the same path as everyone else. But you can't follow the crowd and expect to get God's results. You can't follow everyone else's plan and expect to get God's results. You will only get God's results as you follow His plan, His leading, His purpose, and His direction. I pray that the Lord will open your spiritual eyes so that you can see that there is wealth beyond what you can currently perceive. I pray that you receive the revelation that He is the God of abundance.

REFLECTION

1. What will it take for you to prosper?

2. Do you have courage to go against what everyone else is saying and doing?

3. Are you willing to consult the Lord about all your major purchases?

4. Do you believe the Lord can open your spiritual eyes to see wealth beyond what you can currently perceive?

5. Can you follow everyone else's plan and expect to receive God's results?

MANAGING YOUR RESOURCES LIKE JOSEPH

Money is to be your servant, not your master. Many of us have an unhealthy relationship with money, and so we spend frivolously. It is astounding how many people do not even have saving accounts. A savings account helps you to save money for any future opportunities. Pharaoh was warned in a dream that there would be seven years of abundance followed by seven years of famine. After interpreting Pharaoh's dream, Joseph was promoted to be the second-in-command to Pharaoh. He was tasked with the job of preparing Egypt for the upcoming famine. How did this happen? Joseph took a fifth of the harvest of Egypt during each of the seven years of abundance. Joseph counseled Pharaoh to store 20 percent of those years' harvests. They stored up food during the abundant years, so that the country would not be ruined by the famine.

If we apply the same wisdom as Joseph had, we can avoid experiencing future economic downturns in our finances. If we consider saving a minimum of 20 percent of our income during our years of abundance, we will not be ruined by any "famine" that might befall us. Many of us assume that our greatest problem is a lack of money, when the real issue is actually money management. We spend most of the money that comes into our hands without even thinking about it, and we save little of it, if any at all. How much money did you make last year? How much of that do you still have saved up?

Do not be like Esau, who sold his future for his immediate gratification. He might have been hungry, but he exaggerated when he said that he was "about to die." Isaac was a wealthy man, and Esau was to inherit twice as much as Jacob would, but because he was not able to practice self-control, he lost his birthright.

Many of us exchange a prosperous future for immediate gratification. We go to the store and see an item that we *must* buy, not realizing that investing that money instead could give us double the buying power in the future. Many of us are also only concerned about our own children, but the Word of God instructs us to leave an inheritance for our grandchildren, as well.

REFLECTION

1. Do you have a detailed budget to track your expenses?

2. How much money do you save each month?

3. Are you a faithful tither?

4. Have you traded a prosperous future for immediate gratification?

5. For an entire month, record each purchase in a journal.

HOW TO RECEIVE A PROMOTION LIKE DANIEL

Daniel was so distinguished among the administrators and the satraps that the king planned to set him over the whole kingdom. Daniel worked with such excellence that his work was noticed by the king. Daniel was the type of employee who worked as unto the Lord. Unfortunately, as Daniel increased in favor with his employer, his coworkers became increasingly more jealous of his success. Don't be surprised if your coworkers begin to be jealous of you as you receive more promotions at work. After conducting a thorough investigation of Daniel, "they could find no corruption in him, because he was trustworthy and neither corrupt nor negligent" (Daniel 6:4 NIV).

What is the secret to Daniel's success? The answer is found in Daniel 6: Three times a day he got down on his knees and prayed, giving thanks to his God. Daniel spent his days praying and asking God for help. He was also a great student. He was described as "showing aptitude for every kind of learning, well informed, quick to understand, and qualified to serve in the king's palace" (Daniel 1:4 NIV). Daniel was a learned man: "to these four young men God gave knowledge and understanding of all kinds of literature and learning" (Daniel 1:17 NIV).

REFLECTION

1. Are you distinguished among your peers?

2. Do you work with excellence?

3. What was the secret to Daniel's success?

4. How many times a day did Daniel pray?

5. Daniel was a learned man. What do you spend your time studying?

WHAT WILL IT COST YOU?

This process will cost you a lot of time. Many people have the desire to accomplish the plan of God, but they have not been willing to put in the time. They are not willing to put in the time to develop their gifts. They are not willing to spend time in God's presence. They are not willing to spend time in prayer. They are not willing to spend the time in the Word. They desire to keep following their regular schedules, wasting much of their time on things that don't even matter. They are not willing to set aside some things to focus on the best thing: the plan of God for their lives. They are not willing to set aside their own agendas to take up heaven's agenda, so they have not been able to hear clearly from the Lord.

You cannot keep following your own plan and expect to receive heaven's results. Perhaps you have a desire for the Lord to sanction your own plan. You desire for the Lord to place His stamp of approval on your plan, making it "God-approved." He already has a plan that is "pre-approved," a plan that has been stamped by heaven and whose way has already been cleared for fulfillment. The provision has already been set aside for this pre-approved plan.

If someone offers to build you a house in Arizona, all of the resources required to build that house will be in Arizona. Suppose you decide to relocate to Florida, and you get there expecting to see a fully built house. You become frustrated because you don't see the house there—but the promise you received was for a house in Arizona. What are you doing in Florida? The house is in Arizona! Many of you operate in the same manner: You find yourself in places where the Lord did not direct you to go. You become frustrated and demand that God bless you in a place that is contrary to His perfect will. He has called you to be in a specific place, and that place will be where His grace is found.

REFLECTION

1. Are you willing to invest your time to reach your goals?

2. Are you in the right career path?

3. What do you need to do to hear clearly from heaven?

4. Are you doing exactly what the Lord has directed you to do?

5. Do you believe that you can operate with such wisdom in your life that you know how to respond to each situation?

9

WHAT IS HOLDING YOU BACK?

And there we saw the giants, the sons of Anak, which come of the giants: and we were in our own sight as grasshoppers, and so we were in their sight.

—Numbers 13:33 KJV

What have you always wanted to do, but have been afraid to attempt? Fear is a stressful emotion aroused by an impending threat, whether the threat is real or imagined. Fear has kept many people from being successful. It is a very irrational and destructive force. Too many people suffer from a fear of failure. They refuse to attempt anything at which they are not guaranteed to win. Do not allow the fear of failure to keep you from experiencing success in your life. The Scriptures remind us that God did not give us a spirit of fear: "For the Spirit God gave us does not make us timid, but gives us power, love and self-discipline" (2 Timothy 1:7 NIV).

When Moses sent out the spies to scope out the Promised Land, the spies came back with an "evil report." They allowed fear to cloud their vision. How could they see themselves as "grasshoppers" after they had conquered a mighty nation like Egypt? The men were so full of fear that they said, "We can't attack those people; they are stronger than we are." (Numbers 13:31 NIV). How could they even compare their strength to that of the Canaanites? They were so terrified that they forgot how God had miraculously brought them out of Egypt. They were sizing up the problem against their own size, rather than sizing up the problem against the size of their God. They said, "The land through which we have gone as spies is a land that devours its inhabitants" (Numbers 13:32 ESV). Where did they receive such information? Their overwhelming fear had caused them to make irrational conclusions.

OVERCOMING FEAR

It is hard to believe how these spies could be fearful of the Canaanites, because they themselves were feared by the surrounding nations. They heard about how the Israelites defeated the great nation of Egypt. Moab was filled with dread because of the Israelites; they were terrified of their numbers. Moses sent out twelve spies, and yet only Joshua and Caleb brought back a good report. Caleb had a conquering spirit, and he put his trust in the God who had made the promise. Caleb said, "Let us go up at once and take possession, for we are well able to overcome it" (Numbers 13:30).

The other spies had a "grasshopper" spirit. They saw themselves as small and insignificant. They took their focus off of God's ability to take them to the promised land. But God promised Caleb that he would reach the Promised Land, and Caleb took God at His word. The Lord then said, "Because my servant Caleb has a different spirit and follows me wholeheartedly, I will bring him into the land he went to, and his descendants will inherit it" (Numbers 14:24 NIV). How many of us have stayed in the wilderness because we brought back an "evil report" after spying out our own land? Your "land" is the area that the Lord has promised to give you. He may have promised you a successful business, a successful marriage, or a successful ministry. We should endeavor to be like Caleb and take God at His word. We must have a different spirit from the masses, in order for us to enter our promised land. One day while I was in prayer, this statement came up in my heart: *Don't worry about the giants in the land, you are a giant because the greater one lives in you so go and possess your land.*

REFLECTION

1. How can you overcome fear?

2. What report do you believe about entering your own promised land?

3. Where is your trust?

4. What are some promises that you are believing for?

5. Are you ready to leave the financial “wilderness” behind?

THE FEAR OF LACK

Far too many people suffer from a fear of lack. It can come as a result of misplacing your trust in God. Some people put their trust in the provision rather than in the Provider. There is no shortage in the Kingdom of God. God has resources that you do not even know about. Fear of lack can develop from growing up in an environment of scarcity. Perhaps you did not grow up seeing abundance; you grew up thinking that all you saw was all there was to see. To be free from that mind-set, you must be willing to meditate on the fact that God is a God of multiplication.

Jesus was once preaching to a large crowd in a remote place until evening approached. The disciples asked Him to send the crowds away because they did not have the resources to feed a crowd of over five thousand people. We can read of Jesus' reaction in the book of Matthew:

> *Jesus replied, "They do not need to go away. You give them something to eat." "We have here only five loaves of bread and two fish," they answered. "Bring them here to me," he said. And he directed the people to sit down on the grass. Taking the five loaves and the two fish and looking up to heaven, he gave thanks and broke the loaves. Then he gave them to the disciples, and the disciples gave them to the people. They all ate and were satisfied, and the disciples*

picked up twelve basketfuls of broken pieces that were left over. The number of those who ate was about five thousand men, besides women and children.

—Matthew 14:16–21 NIV

When Jesus took the five loaves and the two fish, He looked up to heaven and gave thanks. Jesus looked up to heaven; He did not look to the number of loaves and fish. He looked upward, to the God who multiplies. And when the disciples distributed the food to the people, as it was being distributed, it multiplied until over five thousand people were fed. Why did the food multiply? Because God is a Creator. He can create anything that you need when you need it. You may think that all that exists is what you can see with your physical eyes, but God is still creating. He is creating new islands, new plants, and new animals.

Each time a person is conceived, God begins the process of creating a brand-new individual. Each person is uniquely different. There are over six billion people on the earth today, and yet none of them have the same fingerprints. God did not stop creating on the seventh day of creation. He rested from all His works, but He did not finish all of His works. He is still creating, and He is not limited by what we see with our physical eyes.

REFLECTION

1. Do you have a fear of lack? What is the root of that fear?

2. What will you choose to meditate on about your finances?

3. Do you believe that God is a creator?

4. Do you feel limited by what you see with your physical eyes?

5. Do you believe that God can multiply your resources?

YOU HAVE CAMPED HERE LONG ENOUGH

As you follow God's plan for your life, you will reach financial levels you have never experienced before. As you follow His will, you will be able to step into new financial territory you never imagined you could reach. The Lord has promised many of us a financial territory, just as He promised the children of Israel to give them the promised land; He has already given you the land! Many of us begin the journey toward our territory, but we are unable to reach our completed destination because we begin to complain along the way. We begin to look at what we see around us, and we begin to pay attention to what others are saying. We focus on the bills that are due and how much the Lord is requiring us to stretch our faith. We start murmuring and we end up in a financial desert.

Far too many people never reach the territory that the Lord promised them. Their promises still stand, as we are now living in a different dispensation of grace. We will not have the same fate as the children of Israel who died in the desert because of their disobedience. The Lord refused to allow them to enter the promised land because of their disobedience. But Jesus died on the cross for our sins; therefore, the promise still stands despite our lack of faith.

There remains a promise for you to enter into another financial realm. You can enter the financial territory that the Lord has promised you. You can pick up the promise any time you are ready to receive its fulfillment in your life. You may have camped in the desert for a while because you were not willing to listen or you were following your own plan. The promise still stands, because the Lord has not abandoned you in the desert of financial lack. He never said you would *never* enter the financial territory that He promised you. You may be required to reach a level of frustration with your current level, however, a level that causes you to say, "God, I have been camping here long enough!"

The children of Israel were camping around a mountain, and the Lord visited them saying, "You have stayed long enough at this mountain" (Deuteronomy 1:6 NIV). As a result, they got up and began to move forward. You have camped around this mountain of financial bondage long enough! You have been around this mountain of financial lack and debt long enough! It is time for you to move forward. It is time for you to enter your promised land. It is time for you to enter God's financial realm. It time for you to enter financial freedom. It is time for you to take the financial territory that the Lord has set aside for you! God's promise still stands, He has not taken away His promise. "God's gifts and his call are irrevocable" (Romans 11:28 NIV). Many have stopped following God's plan and have stopped walking toward the promised land. They stopped walking toward their financial territory.

REFLECTION

1. Where specifically would you like to see yourself financially in one year?

2. Do you believe that you can reach new financial territory?

3. Has God abandoned you in the desert of financial lack?

4. Are you ready to move forward from the “mountain” of financial lack?

5. What are some ways that you can set yourself up for financial success?

PUT GOD'S WORD INTO PRACTICE

It's time for us to start putting God's Word into practice. Many of us know God's Word, but we fail to apply it to our lives. We have spent time studying the Word and confessing the Word, but we have confessed it without much faith. We have not spoken the Word with the expectation that it will become real in our lives. We read the Word like we read any other book. We read it as if we are reading a novel. We fail to understand the creative power that is in the Word of God. We have not confessed the Word with the expectation of seeing it made manifest in our lives. We don't read with the anticipation that we will begin to see it produce results in our lives.

REFLECTION

1. Are you ready to start putting God's word into practice?

2. How much time do you spend studying and confessing the word of God over your life?

3. Do you believe that God's word is the truth?

4. Are you expecting God's promises to be fulfilled in your life?

5. Write down the scriptures that you are confessing over your finances.

JESUS WAS REJECTED

Another fear that holds people back is the fear of rejection. Often this a fear that is learned in childhood. We all have had the experience of sharing our ideas with someone, only to have them be ridiculed. And so we stop coming up with new ideas in order to be accepted by other people. To get along, we learn to go along. Unfortunately, in life there will always be someone who rejects us. If this happens to you, do not be ashamed—you are in good company. The Pharisees rejected Jesus Himself!

> *He was despised and rejected by mankind, a man of suffering, and familiar with pain. Like one from whom people hide their faces he was despised, and we held him in low esteem.*
>
> —Isaiah 53:3 NIV

Jesus knows exactly how you feel because He faced rejection in His life on earth, but He refused to allow the Pharisees to distract Him from His mission. He did not need their approval, because He was so sure of Himself. He knew who He was and where He came from. They rejected Him because they did not understand His purpose. They underestimated His worth and they did not believe in Him.

Unfortunately, you will also be rejected by some people, because they, too, will underestimate your value. They will not understand your purpose, and they will not understand your worth. You are priceless in God's eyes. Learn to look at yourself through your Father's point of view. God takes every insult personally when you are rejected. Allow God to vindicate you as you remain focused on fulfilling your mission in life.

REFLECTION

1. Do you struggle with a fear of rejection? Is that fear of rejection keeping you from pursuing your dreams?

2. How can you overcome your desire to be a people pleaser?

3. Will there be times that you are rejected by others?

4. Who determines your value?

5. Are you willing to stay the course even if you are rejected by some?

TEST OF STEWARDSHIP

Many of us are not prosperous because we never pass the first test. The test of prosperity is stewardship. God will test you with a small amount of money to determine whether you are a faithful steward. As you are proven faithful with a smaller amount, you will be made a steward over much. He will begin to accelerate the amount that you are managing. As you are proven more and more faithful, your next level of stewardship will be doubled, or even tripled, according to your faithfulness. God is a God of multiplication, He does not add—He multiplies. You can either receive multiplication or division, based on your stewardship.

Unfortunately, many Christians believe that they will only become better stewards if they are given a greater amount of money to manage, and yet they are still being unfaithful with the smaller amounts of money they have been given. They never qualify for the multiplication that God has promised them, because they are never found to be faithful over the small amount. They see division instead of multiplication operating in their lives. They see things being divided from them, and their finances keep getting smaller and smaller. They ask, "God, why am I experiencing division instead of multiplication in my life?" The real reason might be because they have not been found to be faithful.

It is never too late to change course. All it takes is one decision. You must be willing to say, "God, I see the error of my ways, and I see where I have been missing it. I will begin to be a better steward of my finances." As you are found to be faithful, God will multiply to you the things that were divided away from you. Your prosperity will come quickly, but you must be found to be faithful. You must pass the test of stewardship.

REFLECTION

1. Have you passed the test of stewardship?

2. Are you being faithful with your finances?

3. How can you become a better steward of your resources?

4. Do you believe that God rewards faithfulness?

5. What will it take for you to change course?

10

BECOMING A GREAT FINANCIAL MANAGER

Whoever can be trusted with very little can also be trusted with much, and whoever is dishonest with very little will also be dishonest with much. So if you have not been trustworthy in handling worldly wealth, who will trust you with true riches? And if you have not been trustworthy with someone else's property, who will give you property of your own?

—Luke 16:10–12 NIV

DESPERATE FOR WISDOM

My traumatic road trip began my search for a plan that would change my financial picture. I earnestly began to seek solutions to my financial challenges. I began to pray like never before, asking God to give me wisdom concerning my finances. One day I called my mother in tears, because we were struggling financially, and she prayed a simple prayer: "Lord, I pray that You would multiply the funds in my daughter's hands, just as You multiplied the loaves and the fishes for the crowds while You were on the earth. Help her to do much with the little that she has."

I believe that the Lord answered her prayer, because shortly thereafter, the Lord began to teach me about financial management. One morning, I was awakened at four o'clock and felt the need to grab a pen and a piece of paper. As I sat there listening, I received a detailed financial plan from the Lord that would forever change the trajectory of my life. He gave me a plan to better manage my finances, a three-part plan I received in prayer. These plans were to be implemented in phases as I was directed to do so by the Lord. The first phase focused on my becoming a great steward of God's resources. I had to learn how to cut costs.

The second phase dealt with the area of saving. I developed a savings plan that forced me to save up a percentage of my income each month. I treated my savings as an expense. I set aside money in a savings account before I would even pay my bills. We continued to tithe throughout this whole process. I spent years learning how to become efficient in managing my finances. The third phase covered investing. I read countless books on investing. I studied both the stock market and the real estate markets. I have studied many different investment vehicles, but I have personally chosen to focus on real estate. I felt that, just like Isaac, I was supposed to stay in that territory and that the Lord would bless us there. We have been very blessed through our investments in real estate.

My husband and I followed a five-year plan in order to overhaul our finances. We implemented changes that would put us in a much better financial position at the end of that time. We were not "keeping up with the Joneses"; we were keeping up with God's plan for us, and that plan put us on the path to debt freedom. Debt comes with tremendous pressure. The Lord took me through a five-year journey of learning about personal finance. I learned to become such a great financial manager that it felt like we had actually received a pay raise!

You must learn how to operate in this financial system yourself; ignorance of the system can be detrimental to your financial health. God never said in His Word that we should not apply sound financial principles. And those principles come from the Word of God—especially from the book of Proverbs. And there are many more financial principles yet to be discovered in the gospels. There are certain financial biblical principles that must be applied in order for you to prosper. As you study and meditate on the Word, these principles will be revealed to you. God has a financial plan for your life. As you follow the leading of the Lord, He will bring you into a "wealthy" place.

REFLECTION

1. Do you need wisdom to prosper?

2. Are you willing to earnestly seek solutions to your financial challenges?

3. Do you believe God can give you a detailed financial plan?

4. Do you have a five-year plan to overhaul your finances?

5. Are you willing to stay the course to follow God's plan?

ARE YOU A GREAT FINANCIAL MANAGER?

When I prayed about my finances, I received an answer that I had not anticipated. I had really expected to receive wisdom on how to increase my income, but instead I received wisdom on how to become a better manager of the resources that I already had. The Lord took me through a journey of learning more about financial management in the Word. I read countless scriptures on how I was expected to be a great financial manager. Matthew 25 tells the story of the parable of the talents. A master was going on a journey, and he called his three servants and left them different levels of wealth to manage. He gave each servant a certain amount of gold, based on each one's ability. When he returned, he found that each one of the servants had doubled his gold—except for the servant who had received one bag of money. That servant was fearful and so he had buried the bag of gold. As a result, his master called him "wicked and lazy."

> *"You wicked, lazy servant! So you knew that I harvest where I have not sown and gather where I have not scattered seed? Well then, you should have put my money on deposit with the bankers, so that when I returned I would have received it back with interest. So take the bag of gold from him and give it to the one who has ten bags. For whoever has will be given more, and they will have an abundance. Whoever does not have, even what they have will be taken from them. And throw that worthless servant outside, into the darkness, where there will be weeping and gnashing of teeth."*

—*Matthew 25:26–30* NIV

There is great insight in this parable on how we should manage our resources. Each servant was expected to increase the master's initial investment. This passage of scripture helped me to understand that it is not the amount that matters as much as how I manage it. God increases the resources of those who manage money well. Most of us might have pitied the servant who only received one bag of gold, but his master actually took away the one bag of gold that he had been given. The master then gave it to the most resourceful servant. This explains why some people continue to increase financially while others lose even the little they had been given. Fear is what kept the servant from becoming a great financial manager, instead causing him to hide the bag of gold. The master said that the least the servant could have done was to gain interest on the initial investment.

God has hired you to be His financial manager. A financial manager is responsible for the financial health of an organization. They produce financial reports, direct investment activities, and develop long-term financial goals. God has brought resources to you according to your ability. Your capacity to manage them determines the amount that you are ultimately given to manage. You are responsible for your own financial health. Would you hire yourself as a financial manager?

REFLECTION

1. Is it possible for you to become a better financial manager?

2. Does God expect you to increase your resources?

3. What is keeping you from being a great financial manager?

4. Are you resourceful?

5. Would you hire yourself as a financial manager? Study Matthew 25

PUT OUT YOUR NETS

God has given you an eternal YES. It's God's good pleasure for you to have good things in life. Jesus found Peter struggling to catch any fish. He was toiling, but he was failing in his endeavor. Jesus spoke a word to him that instantly changed his story.

> *When he had finished speaking, he said to Simon, "Put out into deep water, and let down the nets for a catch." Simon answered, "Master, we've worked hard all night and haven't caught anything. But because you say so, I will let down the nets." When they had done so, they caught such a large number of fish that their nets began to break. So they signaled their partners in the other boat to come and help them, and they came and filled both boats so full that they began to sink.*
>
> —Luke 5:4–7 NIV

Jesus asked Peter to let down his nets, and he obeyed the instructions. As a result, they caught so many large fish that their nets began to break. They called the other partners and filled both boats so full that they were in danger of sinking.

This story illustrates God's method of operation. Peter could have caught just enough fish to supply his needs for one day, but no, he received such an abundance of fish that he had to call his partners in to partake of his blessings. Peter received an abundance of fish because he responded to the words of Jesus. He responded to God's instructions. As you respond to God's will and direction, you will begin to have a "net-breaking" experience. Your nets are your bank accounts. The funds you receive are attached to your purpose. Your abundance will also cause others around you to be blessed. Sometimes we can feel like Peter, in that we have toiled and yet our "nets" are empty. Your bank account may not reflect your years of hard work, but you have to be willing to do as Peter did and say, "Because You say so, I will let down the nets [again]" (Luke 5:5 NIV).

God desires that you prosper in every area of your life. He desires for you to have the good things in life, but He warns you about becoming covetous. *Covetousness* is an "inordinate desire to have what belongs to someone else." Many parents spend hours working so that their children can have the best lives possible; why should we expect to receive anything less from our heavenly Father? We can receive everything that God has ordained for us to have. We must take Him at His Word. The Scriptures state, "Therefore I say to you, whatever things you ask when you pray, believe that you receive them, and you will have them" (Mark 11:24). According to God's Word, we do not have to spend hours praying about our needs, because He knows what we need before we ever ask Him. We must believe that God hears our prayers when we pray.

When we spend too much time reminding God of our needs, we begin to worry instead of believing that He can meet our needs. Jesus never worried about money. He fed five thousand people with just five loaves and two fish. Little is great in the hands of a great God. All resources belong to Him, and He has infinite wisdom on how to increase us financially.

When Jesus and Peter had to pay their taxes, Jesus told Peter to go to the sea and cast out a fish, and it would have their tax payment in its mouth. How many of us would like to pay our taxes this way? God knows how to meet our needs. If He can pay His and Peter's taxes through the mouth of a fish, He can pay your bills, too. Before He can trust you with more resources to manage, though, you must be found to be a faithful manager of His resources.

REFLECTION

1. Where do you feel led to invest your resources?

2. Are you willing to obey God as Peter did?

3. What does the bible say about covetousness?

4. Should we spend all of our time praying about our needs?

5. Does God know how to meet your needs?

SEASON OF UNUSUAL FAVOR

You are entering into a season of favor the likes of which you have never seen before. Things will begin to move, and things will begin to happen for you. Get ready, because the harvest that you have been waiting on is here. I speak peace to your heart, peace to your mind, and peace to your body. God is sending you unusual help. People will want to do things for you that they would not normally do for others.

A few years ago, I was believing God for a mentor in my ministry. I shared my desire with a friend, who rebuked me for believing the impossible. She tried to convince me that no one would be willing to mentor me unless that person had already spent years getting to know me. But I believed that because God knew me, He could connect me with anyone. A couple of weeks later, I was sitting in a meeting conducted by a well-known minister. As she walked past me, she suddenly stopped and asked, “What is the desire of your heart?” I shared with her the dream that God had given me. She looked directly at me and said, “I want to help you accomplish your dream. I would like to start mentoring you.” And thus I was mentored by this amazing woman of God for an entire year. I did not know that minister for months beforehand, but God knew me. It does not matter who you know; it only matters that you know God.

REFLECTION

1. Do you need a mentor? Spend time praying for a mentor.

2. Does it have to take forty years for you to get to your promised land?

3. What do you need to ask God to teach you?

4. Do you believe that God can give you some great ideas?

5. Are you willing to implement the ideas you receive?

WISDOM TEACHES YOU TO INVENT

In 2 Chronicles 26, a king named Uzziah became king at the very young age of sixteen. As long as he sought the Lord, though, God gave him success. How did God prosper Uzziah? God did not send another king to bring piles of gold to Uzziah. He prospered Uzziah through increased wisdom. The king received great ideas from God on how to build towers in Jerusalem and how to dig cisterns and wells. He made machines designed by skillful men for use "on the towers and on the corner defenses so that soldiers could shoot arrows and hurl large stones" (2 Chronicles 26:15 NIV). We are living today in an "idea economy," and new ideas will help you to create greater wealth. Warren Buffett once said, "Indeed, we'll now settle for one good idea a year."

Receiving wisdom from God can literally change your life. Our jobs would become so much easier if we invested time in seeking God for wisdom. George Washington Carver, the famous scientist, asked God to teach him the mystery of the peanut. God answered his prayer, and Carver invented over three hundred products from the peanut. George Washington Carver often said, "The Lord has guided me, and without my Savior I am nothing." Your life will be vastly different a year from now if you will dedicate the time needed to ask God to teach you the mystery of your job, investments, and so on.

REFLECTION

1. How did God prosper Uzziah?

   (Study 2 Chronicles 26:6-15)

2. What can the Holy Spirit teach you?

3. Who is living on the inside of you?

4. Who is the greatest consultant?

5. Are you ready to follow the instructions of the greatest consultant?

EQUIPPED TO FULFILL YOUR PURPOSE

When God asked Moses to build Him a tabernacle, Moses lacked the expertise to undertake such a project. Moses began to seek God for wisdom on how to accomplish the great task of building the Tent of Meeting. The Lord revealed to Moses how He would fulfill the vision.

> *See, I have chosen Bezalel son of Uri, the son of Hur, of the tribe of Judah, and I have filled him with the Spirit of God, with wisdom, with understanding, with knowledge and with all kinds of skills—to make artistic designs for work in gold, silver and bronze, to cut and set stones, to work in wood, and to engage in all kinds of crafts. Moreover, I have appointed Oholiab son of Ahisamack, of the tribe of Dan, to help him. Also I have given ability to all the skilled workers to make everything I have commanded you.*
>
> —*Exodus 31:1–6* NIV

I believe that just as God gave these men from the tribe of Judah wisdom on how to build something that had never been built before, He will do the same for you. God wants to fill you with the same wisdom and knowledge to fulfill your purpose.

The Lord promises to teach you how to prosper. Suppose a benefactor paid the tuition for a student to attend the most prestigious university in the world, and yet the student never showed up for class. Such a student could not be expected to become as learned as the other students who actually showed up for class! Jesus, our Benefactor, has paid for us to attend the class of the Holy Spirit. Jesus promised us that "the Helper, the Holy Spirit, whom the Father will send in My name, He will teach you all things, and bring to your remembrance all things that I said to you" (John 14:26).

Perhaps you have never showed up for class because you have not felt worthy enough to be taught how to prosper. Since the Holy Spirit has promised to teach you, however, you must be willing to put yourself in a position to learn. You learn by listening, by asking questions, and by applying what you have learned. I wasted so much time looking for answers everywhere. I thought that I would find the missing ingredient if I just searched long and hard enough. I read countless of materials searching for ideas on how to prosper, and yet success kept eluding me. I read widely on how to succeed financially, but all of my searches just came up empty. After years of wasted effort, I finally came to understand that the answers were inside of me. I had wasted so much time looking for gold to mine externally, not knowing that I should have been mining internally.

I wasted time looking externally, when I should have been looking inwardly. The Creator of the universe is living on the inside of you in the Person of the Holy Spirit. You must take the time to listen to His counsel. Many people spend money hiring external financial consultants, and they do serve a purpose, but we actually have the greatest Consultant living on the inside of us. All you have to do is ask Him to reveal the mysteries of the financial system to you, just as He revealed the mysteries of the peanut to George Washington Carver. He can supernaturally teach you how to start a business. You must be willing to listen to the Consultant.

He is not only your spiritual consultant, but He can also be your business consultant and your financial consultant. Will you show up for the class?

BONUS QUESTIONS FOR ENTREPRENEURS

"Thinking is hard work; that's why so few do it."
Albert Einstein

1. What type of business can you start with the resources that you have? Ask God to reveal it to you. (Study 2 Kings 4)

2. How much money will you need to start your business?

3. Do you need to form strategic alliances for your business?

4. Where will your business be located?

5. What is your motivation for wanting to start your own business?

6. What is your vision for your business?

7. Who is your target market?

8. What are your short-term and long-term goals for your business?

9. How is your product or service different from others in the market?

10. How well you do know your market? Who are your competitors?

11. What is the demand for your business? How do you plan to close the knowledge gaps?

12. How do you plan to market your business?

13. How is success defined in your business?

14. How long will you dedicate to doing a feasibility study before launching into business? (Study Luke 14:28)

15. When should you launch your business? (Pray about timing)

A PRAYER OF BLESSING FOR YOU

Father, I pray for the person reading this book right now. I pray that each reader will experience financial breakthrough as they read this book. I pray that this book is the catalyst for a change in their finances. May they be surrounded with favor as a shield. They will be favored, and others will want to do for them what they would not normally do for others. I pray that you would begin to teach them how to prosper. May you bring them the best opportunities.

May they not lack in any area of their lives, and certainly not in their finances. May you cause them to be the head and not the tail. May their eyes be opened to discover new investment opportunities. I pray that they will never miss any good opportunity. May they give liberally to see the Kingdom of God advanced. As they sow into the Kingdom of God, I pray that it would be given back to them, pressed down, shaken together, and running over. Father, I ask that You would show Yourself strong on behalf of each person who is reading this book. I declare each one blessed, and I thank You for fulfilling that word. May they abide in God's mercy for the rest of their lives.

I pray that just as Caleb could conquer his mountain, they would also begin to conquer their own financial mountains. I pray that this book touches their lives. May it cause them to enter into a financial realm that they have not been able to tap into yet. I pray that they will begin to increase supernaturally. I also pray for those who have been experiencing a financial blockage, who have been held back financially. May they begin to prosper financially. May they begin to possess their promised land because they have a conquering spirit like Caleb. They are well able to conquer their own territory, and so they must go and take their territory.

I look forward to hearing your own testimony!

JESUS PAID THE ULTIMATE PRICE

God loves you so much that He sent His one and only Son to die for you. God knew every sin that you would ever commit, and yet He still chose to love you. There is no greater love than what He has bestowed upon you. If you have never accepted Jesus as your personal Lord and Savior, pray the prayer below so that you can accept the price that was paid for you:

"Father, I believe that Jesus is the Son of God. I believe that He died on the cross for my sins and I receive Him now as my personal Lord and Savior."

ABOUT THE AUTHOR

Junise Moise is a writer, teacher, and speaker who inspires others to apply the Word of God to their lives so that they can experience success in every area of their lives. She is the wife of an amazing man of God and a mother of four future world-changers. Junise was born in the country of Haiti, and she emigrated to the United States at the tender age of ten. At the age of sixteen, she had an encounter with God, and her life began to transform. She received the call of God to preach at the age of eighteen years old. She spent many years running from this call, until she encountered a life-changing situation that prompted her to say "yes" to the calling on her life. She has a bachelor's in finance from Northeastern State University. She is also a graduate of Rhema Bible Training Center in Broken Arrow, Oklahoma. Junise has served as a teacher of the Word in various women's ministry. She is the co-founder of Moise Ministries International, an evangelistic ministry that reaches the lost and hurting. Her passion is to empower women to boldly walk in the authority of Christ. She has spent years studying the Bible so that she could teach others how to apply it to their lives. Junise and her family live in their promised land of Phoenix, Arizona.

Junisemoise.org

Made in the USA
Monee, IL
09 May 2024

58260870R00094